BY
HER
OWN
HAND

Passionate Attachments: Fathers and Daughters in America Today

Daughters and Mothers: Mothers and Daughters

Women: Body and Culture

BY HER
OWN HAND

MEMOIRS OF A SUICIDE'S DAUGHTER

SIGNE
HAMMER

SOHO

Published by Soho Press, Inc.
853 Broadway
New York, NY 10003

Library of Congress Cataloging-in-Publication Data
Hammer, Signe.
By her own hand: memoirs of a suicide's daughter/Signe Hammer
p.   cm.
ISBN 0-939149-49-4:
1. Hammer, Signe.   2. Mothers and daughters—United States-
Biography,3. Suicide victims—Family relationships.   I. Title.
CT275.H3537A3   1991
937.9'092—dc20   91-8364
[B]   CIP
Manufactured in the United States
10   9   8   7   6   5   4   3   2   1

Book design and composition by
The Sarabande Press

For Dr. Marjorie Taggart White
With Love and Gratitude

1	The Kitchen	3
2	Idle Speculations	13
3	The Lost Tribes: A Portrait of My Mother and Her House	24
4	Cunning Little Compartments: A Portrait of My Father and His Railroad	36
5	Norwegian Wood	44
6	German-American Relations	59
7	In the Realm of the Senses	76
8	The Home Front	87
9	Travels in *Arabia Deserta*	101
10	After the Peace, the Cold War	119
11	Hiroshima, mon Amour	137
12	The Book of Ezekiel	146
13	The Second Coming	165
14	Final Analysis	187

BY
HER
OWN
HAND

ONE

The Kitchen

I'M VERY young, my first time at the theater. Mary Poppins has taken the Banks children to tea at the home of some friends of hers, and while they sit on the late-Victorian furniture it rises, gently, toward the ceiling. The Banks children's eyes bug out, my eyes bug out, the production is a hit. And they eat real fruitcake.

I know the fruitcake is real because we go onstage afterward and I take a good look at it. It immediately suggests to me the possibility of a whole life onstage, where everyone could see me but I would be set off from them, in a magical space where I could perform magical acts, like flying. Yet I could eat real fruitcake. The image dazzles.

At home I immediately start to draw pictures for plays, hanging the pictures up on my little red wooden wheelbarrow and delivering the narration, like a slide show. As soon as I learn to write, I become the school playwright and star performer. At will I can change my geography, my time, my family, my age, my sex.

When I was nine, though, something happened that put an end to this activity. In the spring of 1950, right before Easter, resurrection time, my mother decided to go in the other direction. She committed suicide.

Her method was simple and effective. One night, when my father was away and we children had gone to bed, she set up the ironing board in front of the open oven, turned on the gas, lay down on the ironing board, and waited for the gas to do its work.

I don't know how she got herself onto the ironing board; she was five-foot-six or so, according to one photograph I have in which she is posed in front of a measuring scale, probably for an army PX I.D. I don't actually remember the ironing board; it is a detail supplied by one of my brothers, in the only conversation we ever had about our mother's death. We were adults by then, and he had had a few drinks, so I suppose it is the truth.

At some point after she lay down, and probably after she died, there was an explosion; she had forgotten, apparently, to turn off the refrigerator, and some spark ignited the gas. Or was that part of her plan, to dispose of the gas so none of us would be overcome by it when we found her?

She hadn't wanted to take me with her. My room, tiny and high-ceilinged, was right above the kitchen, in the back of the house. There was an old-fashioned iron grill in the floor to allow warm kitchen air to flow through. It had been covered over because I couldn't sleep with people down there clattering dishes and arguing, but she must have wanted to make sure. So when it was time to go to bed she asked me whether, as a treat, I wanted to sleep in the guest room, in the front of the house next to the room she shared with my father.

She knew I would accept. I hated my room, set apart from everyone else's. My three brothers slept in a cluster of bedrooms on the third floor that we called the boys' dormitory. It had been a few years since I had been so frightened by my nighttime isolation that I had braved the black wells of the back and front stairs to get to the safety of my parents' bed, but I still loved sleeping in the guest room. It felt like I belonged somewhere, with people.

When she came to tuck me in that night she hugged me long and hard, wrapping her arms around my shoulders and lifting me up to her. She held me as if she were reminding herself of what it felt like. When she went back downstairs, she left the door open a few inches so I could see the light from the hall.

The explosion hit my sleep as a sentence in a dream: "The books fell on the floor." I woke up hearing my brothers pounding down the back stairs, caught a glimpse of flying pajamas. I went wide-eyed next door, and saw that the bed was still made, as if it were daytime. I knew something was all wrong, and followed my brothers down to the kitchen.

Erik was out in the driveway yelling FIRE!, his voice cracking a little in panic. Hal was in the kitchen, standing over my mother, feeling for a pulse. She was dressed in her old brown house slacks and a red sweater.

I walked several hesitant steps into the kitchen, over ash

that had been paint, seared from the ceiling and cabinets. I noticed a little blue line of flame along the wooden counter. That must have been the moment I knew my mother was dead, because I stopped, backed up, and stood in the doorway, unable to move.

A DEAD body is like a black hole in space; it sucks everything in and gives nothing back. You can't take your eyes off it, because you can't believe it's not going to move. But it denies you; it's absent.

I had seen death once before. The death I knew was that of a cat, curled up in its usual place on a bit of carpet at the foot of the cellar stairs. It, too, looked stiff, angular; the form of cat was there, but the thing that had made it cat was gone. It had become like an old dustcloth rinsed, wrung out, and left to dry to a stiff twist. I thought it could happen to me, anytime.

We buried the cat in a cardboard box in the dirt by the kitchen foundation wall, where my mother grew a few box bushes. Afterward I felt cut off from myself. The cat's death short-circuited the connection that had gone through its juicy little body, its purr, its soft fur, that were all something like love. I resented this disconnection, but I felt a panicky helplessness, too.

The cat and my mother had become untouchable.

AFTER A while, neighbors appeared, and I was sent upstairs to my own room, to grope in the smoke for my bathrobe.

Nobody thought it was strange to send me on this errand; it was a reflex, to behave as though nothing had happened. I worried about my hamster in his cage in the basement, but I was not allowed to go down and get him. Nobody hugged me; nobody hugged anyone, then or later. (As far as I know, the only one who ever mourned, besides myself, was my father: Not long afterward, I heard him roaring through the empty rooms of the first house we moved to after the suicide, bellowing AGNES! at the top of his lungs. He thought he was alone, but I was sitting on a little bench in the kitchen entryway, just outside the screen door, and I heard. I didn't recognize my father; his grief was terrifying. He never knew that I knew; it was one more thing that could never be acknowledged.)

The neighbor's wife herded us from the house. As we turned from the driveway onto the street, I looked back; firemen were carrying a stretcher down the one wide step from the front porch. The figure on it was draped with a brown blanket; even invisible, it had the same stiff, mysterious stillness it had had on the ironing board.

YOU CAN do things with your mind. You can speed things up, surround the suicide with words, contain the explosion, tidy up the kitchen. Your mind can repaint the walls and ceiling, install new, fireproof metal cabinets, and lay scorchproof linoleum on the floor. In the mind's kitchen, the squat, ancient refrigerator, with its cooling coils in a kind of turban on top, capable of generating a spark, perhaps, as they cycle on and off, is pasted over with a tall, cool, sleek rectangle. The electric oven, high up on the wall, can do no worse than scorch the meat. In this desperate kitchen my mother can still move efficiently between her red tin recipe box and the oven, baking her bread, her pies, her cakes, posing as the sanitized kitchen goddess, the star of our family mythology.

But the mind knows she was never really like that. She was the full Fury, the dark side of hell, as cold and calculating a witch as ever stirred a cauldron. All the mind's imaginings can't paste over her black act. Her suicide is seared into my brain; the burned kitchen with its body remains, an after-image, flashing along the optic nerve no matter what other reality enters my eye.

THE NIGHT before, she had sat in the wing chair in the living room, her eyes swimming with tears, staring straight ahead at nothing. Frightened, as always, by her remoteness and her desperation, I had walked hesitantly into the room and stopped. I brought good news; Hal, my middle brother, the oldest at home, had decreed that we children would stop fighting at the dinner table. We would do the dishes every night. It was important to tell my mother about this because a few minutes earlier, when our usual supper-time quarrels had begun (my father was working in New York, coming home only on weekends), she had stood up and announced to my youngest brother and I, the bitter-est arguers, "If you two don't stop fighting, I'm going to kill myself."

And now she had.

BY HER OWN HAND

ONE OF my cousins once told me that my mother had carefully planned her death. They found a scrapbook, he said, in which she had kept clippings of successful suicides; the kind of article in which, after telling when and where the body was found, the journalist describes how it was done. My mother had outlined a number of methods, meticulously listing the equipment necessary, if any, and the steps to be taken, in turn. Like a recipe: Blow out pilot light. Turn temperature indicator to BROIL. Place meat on ironing board, uncovered.

I never saw this scrapbook, but I have imagined it almost as many times as I have imagined myself lying down in my mother's place in front of the oven. One night early in the second semester of my sophomore year in college, when my father and stepmother had just moved into the city and strangers were living in our house, cooking in my mother's kitchen, I left the campus in the middle of the night. I was intent on going home to her kitchen, to lie down on the table or whatever was available. Until then, I couldn't sleep. Sleep felt too private; you reclaim yourself and forget the other. I couldn't forget her, not for one second.

When I first went away to college, I forgot her for whole months. I made friends, I fell in love, I was happy. I could act more or less like a person who really was an adolescent female, with sexual desires and fantasies and juicy urges to live. I dreamed of touching other people, of looking them in the eyes, even smiling.

But however many connections I made, when I went home her death short-circuited me. During Thanksgiving vacation of my sophomore year, I lay upstairs on Hal's bed, imagining myself committing suicide with one of his guns. I thought of using a little .22 repeating rifle, but when I looked in the drawer of his bedside table, where he kept his ammunition, I couldn't find the right shells. So I went downstairs to Thanksgiving dinner. Nobody asked where I had been.

During that vacation I slept, as I had for years, in my mother's bedroom, on her bed, under her bedspread—my father's idea of an inheritance appropriate to a daughter. At three, at five, I had dreamed of this, but in those dreams she was there, too. Now there was just myself, her afterimage.

Her suite of bedroom furniture was Cuban mahogany. Its lines were simple, even severe: a double bed with a headboard that sloped gently up to a shallow peak in the middle, a tall bureau, and a rectangular dressing table with straight legs, one drawer, and a three-piece mahogany-framed mirror that made a triptych out of anyone who sat in front of it.

My mother's jewelry boxes had been given to me. They looked as though they belonged on the mahogany surface of her dressing table: a heavy, rectangular box of inlaid metal, a little baroque silver ring box, the enameled wood box my father had brought her from Persia during World War II. The sandalwood box he brought me from the Philippines, with elephants carved in relief, looked all right, too, but the big, padded, pale-blue-plastic teenager's jewelry box he and my stepmother had given me, stamped in gilt and lined in shell-pink satin, looked grotesque.

My father and stepmother had also added a huge, claw-and-ball-footed desk for me to write and do my homework on; a bookcase; and an immense expanse of bulletin board on which, over the years, I dutifully tacked football-game favors, corsages, and movie-star photos. But the room was never mine. I was a ghost in it. When I opened the closet door, I always half expected to see my mother's shoes in the door rack, her tweed suits and wool dresses hanging from the rod.

At four, in Fort Wayne, Indiana, I had had a nosebleed on her bed. I had lain right on top of the white cotton summer bedspread, with the design picked out in pink chenille, but somehow the spread had survived. It was on her bed the night she killed herself.

All through my adolescence, I had nightmares in my mother's bed. I would float in a black sea of static; my head would drop back and suddenly I would fall away into nothingness. Or I would blunder into a dark room, alive with coppery static. Gradually I could make out huge figures sitting in giant armchairs, their knees looming above me, their heads disappearing in the crackling electrical atmosphere. Their outlines were fuzzy, like metal filings clustered by a magnetic field. They were giants of eternity, of judgment, and I was rooted in front of them. I could feel my outline blurring and coming apart.

The summer between my freshman and sophomore years in college, I lived at home and tried to hold myself together. At my job in an insurance company in Philadelphia, I weeded the files of folders on elderly, long-retired clerks with names like Thelma and Mae. In my spare time I read *The Outsider,* a book about the isolation and madness of Nijinsky and other artists and visionaries. I felt myself to be an outsider and a visionary because on some level I had known that my mother was going to kill herself. I believed that if I could be a genius, like Nijinsky, I could save myself for a while, but that, like Nijinsky, I was doomed.

By the time I got back to school, I was in a panic. My rational mind was functioning brilliantly, writing papers, taking tests, getting A's. But inside my head everything was moving too fast; the suicide kept threatening to explode. Outside, there was this cold, slow-moving reality of classes and meals and running into people in the bathroom. I grew afraid to meet people because of what I was carrying around inside me.

I began to stay up all night, sleeping during the day, cutting classes. At dinnertime, when everyone else was downstairs in the dining room, I would roam the dormitory corridors, ghostlike, looking for pills in the dark rooms. I put together a mixed bag and one night I took them. At some gray hour of the morning I woke, cold, sweating, and sick.

The windows of the dormitory were too low for jumping, the ground below too soft for landing. In my mind, I worked my way into my mother's kitchen. When I left the dormitory, I wasn't exactly planning to repeat her act. I didn't really want to kill myself; I thought I was supposed to. I had in mind something like a religious ritual, in which the living sacrifice is immolated as the god, who is brought to life in the body and blood of the sacrifice. In me, her torment continued; if I could finally take her place, it would be as every one of us in the family had wanted it all those years; as if nothing had ever happened.

TWO

Idle Speculations

IN MY dreams, I go back to that house all the time. It's always empty, except for me; everyone else has just left, or I'm waiting for them to come back. I hang around upstairs, or in the dining room, or just outside the kitchen, healed now and white. I never dream of it ruined.

Often, there are strange visitors outside, carloads of men and women pulled into the semicircular driveway, looking expectantly for signs of life. They occupy the space, as if they belong there. Invisible, I check out the front porch. Did I lock the front door? The side door? The basement door? The house has too many openings.

Sometimes, in my dream, I float down the silent, empty lanes of the neighborhood. At any moment, if I reveal myself, or am revealed, something will happen—a door will open, someone will come out, discover me. I don't know whether it is fear or desire that propels me. Fear makes me invisible, but desire sends me out of the house.

Sometimes I dream that I'm following the stalker, the possible rapist. I imagine myself becoming him; I walk out the side door, down the side-porch steps and onto the stones and gravel and dead leaves of the carriageway, with its two ruts curving downhill to the old brick carriage house. I follow in the stalker's footsteps as he cuts away from the drive at the point where it turns at the corner of the house. I step through the gap in the hedge made by generations of dogs and children, around the beaten dirt pit where my brother Erik and I used to burn the paper trash. We would make complex constructions of boxes and bags and watch the black char spread as the little flames curled up the cardboard, feeling the sudden rush of heat as a paper bag caught, burned, and, lightened to ash, buoyed by hot air, abruptly rose above our heads to sail away in a cross breeze.

Below the firepit, a tangle of weeds, poison ivy, dead leaves, raspberry bushes hairy with reddish, flexible spines. (We called them wineberries; our mother paid us by the quart for picking them.) Here there is a larger, shallower pit, partially grown over, that has been dug for a fort and abandoned. The stalker pauses where the hill flattens out, his black cowboy boots planted firmly in the poison ivy. He is tall and thin, his long legs in black pants, his hipbones holding up his worn black belt with the tarnished pewter buckle. He wears a black silk shirt open at the neck, with a black neckerchief tied on one side. His hair is black too, and he squints pitilessly as he surveys his terrain. This is the place to which he will drag me, shielded from neighbors and passersby, a soft bed of leaves in the shallow pit, a place to roll and gambol when, touched by me, he becomes my lover.

Over the ground the mauve smoke of old fires, old leaves, crumbling shards of old blue slate.

MY SHOCKED relatives probably threw out the suicide scrapbook. I wish they had kept it; I would like to be able to retrace my mother's route to the oven, find out why she chose that way instead of, say, carbon monoxide from the car, or a quick shot from one of my middle brother's guns. I think it was because the kitchen was the seat of whatever power she felt she had in that house. If she were going, at long last, to leave my father, she would do it there. It was a neat trick: She would leave, but stay; slip out through the eye of the goddess, which would blink once and steal her from our sight, from our plans, from our terrible needs.

SHE HAD considered an alternative. My uncle once told me that she had gone to her mother-in-law, my grandmother, a small, patrician woman who sat on her Sheraton sofa with her straight back never touching the upholstery. My grandmother offered my mother coffee. After my mother said what was on her mind, my grandmother looked at her through her gold-framed pince-nez and said, "In this family, we do not divorce."

Between that meeting and her suicide, my mother spoke to a friend of hers, the mother of the girl my oldest brother later married. It was my sister-in-law who, years later, told me how my mother had driven her mother home one afternoon. When she pulled into the driveway, my mother leaned back, her hands still on the wheel, and asked, "Do you ever feel that you just can't take it anymore?"

This isn't much to go on. There have, of course, been family speculations: One of my brothers once said that he wondered whether our father had taken a mistress during the war, and our mother had found him out. My stepmother and my aunt believed my mother had a terrible secret that she was too noble to tell any of us: she was dying anyway, of cancer. Even I have wondered whether an early menopause contributed to a deep, unassuageable despair.

There is one fact: My uncle, my father's only brother, once told me that my mother chose to kill herself on the anniversary of the day she had promised to marry my father.

A SUICIDE stops time. Before it happens, it is unimaginable. When it does happen, it feels unreal, out of time. Illness prepares you for death, and you can explain an accident. You can rail away at fate, or get angry at the other person, or even at the person who was killed, for being drunk at the wheel, or careless. You can be stunned, but you can grieve.

You can't get angry at a suicide, and you can't grieve. If you ask *why?* any possible answer seems to implicate you. Your questions become guilty: *How did I fail her? What could I have done?*

No one wants to deal with these questions. To avoid them, the family provides the suicide with conventionally dramatic occasions, like menopause or adultery or cancer. If my mother sacrificed herself to spare us the pain of her cancer, she was beyond human frailty—beyond our failures of sympathy, of empathy, of word, of act. If she was holy and perfect, we were off the hook, our guilt redeemed.

We were also sane, and so was she. A suicide is an extreme act. Without a motive, it seems a defeat of the self, a pointless punishment—incomprehensible, perhaps even mad. And the implications of madness are as disturbing as those of motive: *If she was mad, what were we? What are we now?*

What we are is this: Of her four children, one is manic-depressive; on lithium, the classic drug. The other three of us are, to varying degrees, chronically depressed. All of which could be the work of an inherited trait or disease. And that raises the question whether depression as a mere set of malfunctioning neurons, with no relation to circumstance, could have driven my mother to kill herself.

I suppose that, in theory, it could have; a clinical depression can make the act of living feel too painful to go on with. But my mother's suicide clearly had great meaning for her; she chose its form and its time so carefully, carried it out so well. I think her depression became unbearable as her life became unbearable—because she no longer perceived any possibility of a future inside or outside of marriage. To stay alive is to project yourself into the future every second; to lose your future is a kind of death-in-life.

Today, of course, she would probably have gotten a divorce. But in 1949 or 1950 it wasn't easy for a middle-aged woman with four children to initiate divorce proceedings, especially if nobody in her family was backing her up. To prove cause, she would have had to charge my father with something like adultery, which he probably had never committed. It would have been very difficult for her to contemplate, much less go through, the messy, tawdry business of accusations, the establishment of proof.

She wouldn't have liked the image the world would pin on her after she slammed the door, either. She cared, almost desperately, for the proprieties, but divorced women were called *divorcées,* a term suggestive of wickedness and irresponsibility, with definite overtones of promiscuity.

Marriage was still how women made a living. As a single parent—almost unheard of in the middle classes at that time—what would she have done for money? She was probably too much of an idealist to plan on alimony, and even if she had thought of it she may, given my father's notorious stinginess, have despaired of the possibility of actually receiving it. She certainly would not have looked forward to continuing to be financially dependent on him. But she hadn't held a job in twenty years. There weren't any support groups to help her invent a résumé and role-play a job interview. "Life experience" had no currency in the marketplace. It must have seemed to her that if she dropped out, she'd be gone.

I don't think any of this is enough to explain why she chose death, though. They may all be factors, but next to them the word *suicide* still sounds extreme, suggests something that takes place not in what we like to think of as daily life but in another dimension, in which the chain of cause and effect has gone awry, so that apparently ordinary acts or situations lead to consequences that are tragic beyond bearing. The dimension in which Clytemnestra operated, and Medea. And my mother.

Who was, in her own way, a tragic heroine too, victim and villain both, like her great predecessors. Revenge was certainly on her mind; her suicide ruined my father's career. He never quite forgave her for that; it must have seemed like another strand in the web of a fate he set himself to deny at all costs.

High tragedy may seem improbable in an age of quantum mechanics, when things happen randomly all over the universe: Identify a photon, and the next second you have no idea where it is. Take a cruise, and you wind up being shot by terrorists and thrown overboard before your wife's eyes. Take a plane, and a bomb explodes under your seat, ejecting you without a parachute, to plummet into the sea next to an equally astonished infant.

But this suicide, like all real tragedies, was a family affair. The Greeks and Shakespeare understood what we deny; that, in families, actions almost always have a reason. Fate is tied to character, and even the gods are led by their vices, their desires, and their weaknesses.

In a family, lives are tangled together, so that parents confuse each other, their sons, and their daughters with their own pasts. The present can reverberate so strongly with the cries of the parents' former selves that a betrayed wife can come to see nothing but doom where an outsider sees something simple, rational, and finite—a decision to move to another place, say. An option. Nothing very extreme, certainly.

And all the while, the futures of the sons and daughters are created or canceled, depending on whether their parents allow them to escape or suck them into their games, so that the parents' despair endures as the children's painful, eternal present.

Although I don't think my mother meant to include me in her revenge, she and I were hopelessly intertwined by our gender and my youth, and by the peculiar ways in which I served her needs and, later, the family's. She had seen in me a mirror of herself, and so had always seemed to me to be my particular responsibility. To my brothers, who were boys and older, her suicide meant a shock, a loss, an interruption, feelings of guilt and anger to be denied; to me, it meant the end of any sense of myself as a separate person.

Of course, after all these years I realize intellectually that my mother's act may have had very little, perhaps nothing at all, to do with me. Yet I was, willy-nilly, deeply embroiled in her life, in secret aspects of her character that may have revealed themselves only in what happened between us. So each one in the family had a secret life with her, each child was shaped by her. And, being shaped, imagined being the shaper.

In a tragedy, chance doesn't intervene. Nothing distracted Artemis; the wind didn't shift, and Agamemnon didn't sail for Troy without sacrificing his daughter and provoking his wife to vengeance. My father wasn't suddenly told he would not be transferred after all. None of us children got up in the middle of the night and went down to the kitchen for a glass of milk, and found my mother, and opened all the windows, and saved her life.

The questions haunt me, past all the family speculations: Could any of us—myself, for instance—have saved her, and was one of us—myself, for instance—therefore responsible for the fact that she died? Or for the fact that she turned on the gas in the first place?

If I can't let go of these questions, neither could my father or brothers, despite their denials. Suicide is self-murder, and murder engenders the desire for a punishment of mythic dimensions, some primitive form of vengeance, such as taking the murderer's life. In a suicide, though, the murderer takes her own life. And since she's also the victim, she is blameless. So the desire to judge, to punish, and to control leads inexorably back to us, the survivors.

My family wanted simply to deny everything, but there I was, the spitting image of my mother according to everyone who had known her, and growing to look more like her every day. While I was around, none of us could forget her. They had to do something with me. As it turned out, I served their purpose as much as I threatened it. My guilt and their denial were a perfect fit. Together, we created a little household theater in which it appeared that nothing played—nor ever had played—but the most innocuous domestic sitcoms. If my mother had annihilated herself, my father would annihilate her act—bury it under life as usual.

What's buried, airtight, in tomb or peat bog or brain, is out of time, preserved forever; old guilts, old enmities, old terrors. All myths intact, the image in the child's eye unchanged. If these things are dug up, restored to time, some will disintegrate from light and air. Others will serve the truth, or what of it can be reconstructed from potsherds, tools, bones, and scraps of cloth.

How much of what I write here can be the truth? From

my point of view, all of it: both what I remember and what I re-create from biographical and historical fact and by digging into my own psyche, where my mother lies buried as deep as her deed.

It's now well-known that memory is unreliable, that neither reconstruction nor memoir can exactly re-create reality. The observer's presence alters the arrangement of the universe; neither archaeologist, astronomer, nor poet stands on neutral ground or holds an objective point of view. But as far as that goes, we're all fictions, continually imagining ourselves and each other, providing running continuity for our lives that might easily be challenged by a stern observer. I've corrected myself as much as possible in matters of fact, but the subjective experience is what shapes the memory and the person, and this is not *Rashomon*. I'm writing not just to make sense of my life, an honorable enough goal for an artist, but to restore myself to it, and it to me.

It's another truism that each child of the same parents lives in a different family (although when my father died there were many hints dropped that none of us had ever found him an easy man to deal with). The mother I'm looking for is my mother, just as the suicide I've described is the one I experienced, and what happened afterward is what I remember. I know that my brothers have some memories in common with mine, but insofar as I have ever been able to discuss it with them, I also know that for them the suicide meant something very different, just as their mother, although contained within the same skin, was not quite the same as mine.

If I can learn something of who my mother was—and of

who we all were, both before and after the suicide—I will
discover some answers to the most elusive and most difficult
question of all: what brought her to it? The "why?" that is
the first question everyone asks after a suicide and is the
least likely to be answered, so quickly is it obscured by more
pressing questions of family politics and personal interest.

The way the family reacted to my mother's suicide was
perfectly consistent with the way it had behaved when her
live body was there at its center. Her act transformed us as
radically as a violent revolution can change the shape of a
culture. But in the culture that emerges from the chaos of a
revolution you can usually find elements of the prerevolu-
tionary past, transformed into the ideological image of the
new. Even after a millennium or so you can sometimes still
find cut stone from the original temples in the foundation
walls of state institutions, or notice, embroidered in a wall
hanging, motifs that turn up woven into fragments of ancient clothing or incised on small stones once used for
counting animals or measuring grain.

We're an ancient culture now; the family lives entombed
inside the heads of my three brothers and myself. My
brothers, who want to leave it there, think me peculiar,
obsessed—possibly even mad. Perhaps I am. I write to
excavate my mother, her act and its aftermath from the
layers of myth and ritual, cant and oblivion, that have
preserved and obscured them all these years. I disappeared
under the same layers of debris and kitchen midden that
buried her. If I can find us both—the Great Goddess and
my child-self, in whose eyes the Goddess lives—I will be
able, at last, to let them both go and take up my own life.

THREE

The Lost Tribes:
A Portrait of My Mother
and Her House

M Y MOTHER was a formal person. Since she killed
herself, she has become a shadowy figure in my
dreams, but I can look at her in photographs, standing
behind a row of us children. They are black-and-white
photographs, taken outside; we children squint up, blindly,
into the lens and the sun. My mother, copper-glinting
brown hair and green-blue eyes (my hair; my eyes) muted to
shades of gray, does not squint, but her smile seems careful.
Certain tribespeople still object to being photographed
because they believe that the camera can capture their souls.
Our civilized version of this belief is that snapshots show
what people hide, even from themselves: how they feel
about themselves and the people who share the photograph
with them, how they all really relate to each other.

In the photos of my family, none of us quite touch. In a

picture taken not long before her suicide, my mother stands beside my oldest brother Arno, a college freshman. They both look front and center, and their arms drop straight down at their sides like those of soldiers standing at attention. My mother seems to look forthrightly into the camera, but she is not telling everything about herself; she is preserving her soul.

She wears a tweed suit with shoulder pads, and a felt hat with a narrow brim turned up sharply on one side to display a little feather. My cousin, the painter, always said my mother had taste in clothes, and she did. Buying clothes, she was as sure of herself as she was in the kitchen. She would try on suit after suit while I crouched in a corner of the fitting room, fascinated and bored at the same time. She liked earth tones—browns, dark oranges, dark greens—but she understood a more urban sophistication: a black-and-white houndstooth-check suit with a flash of red at the shoulder, or a black dress with a short jacket that had a maroon panel on one side, worn with a maroon bag and heels. Her shoes hung in rows on the rack on the inside of her closet door: rich brown walking shoes, wine-colored sling-backs with open toes and high heels.

It's not easy for me to describe her physically, even though everyone who knew her has always told me I look exactly like her, and I myself can see that physically I take after her. She was less than two inches shorter than I am, large-boned and strong, a good swimmer. When she was thin, as she was at the end, she looked rawboned, like one of the Appalachian women in Walker Evans's photographs for *Let Us Now Praise Famous Men*. She had the same high cheekbones, too, but her eyes were soft and veiled; although they were often full of pain they didn't have the same fierce glare, the rage to survive.

She was attentive to details; a perfectionist. She had grown up in an arts-and-crafts studio: Her mother was a potter, her father a woodcarver, printmaker, and all-around commercial artist as well as a painter and sculptor. As a girl, she had mastered the magic of the wheel, the thick wet gray mound of clay opening in front of her, turning, turning, slithering up slick and snakelike as she played it between fingers and thumbs. But when she grew up she opted for housewifery. She decided to put all her talent and training into things like sewing little smock dresses for me, or making Christmas ornaments from construction paper or scraps of cloth and wood.

She liked being bent over her work; she could be wholly engaged by the task of wrapping a parcel. Her swift, delicate fingers touched everything with the same gentle dexterity, making it do exactly what she wanted it to. She would tie up the rose bushes or fold clean sheets with equal solicitude.

In a good mood, she approached us children the same way. When she bathed me and washed my hair she was nimble-fingered and gentle; she always told me to close my eyes before the vinegar rinse. But she never caressed me. She kept the touching to a minimum: no slow, sensual licks with the washcloth; never a lapse into silliness and tickling.

When we were sick, she was as competent as a good nurse; her hands could soothe with cold compresses, stroke on salve or pick bits of cinder delicately from flesh, as they did when, at eight, shirtless, I took a header on the cinder track behind the high school. Once, when I had done some kind of damage to my arm, pulled a muscle perhaps, she rubbed it with salve and wrapped it in the heating pad. I kept saying it hurt long after it was healed, her touch felt so good.

My brother Hal turned out to be the only one of us children who was really good with objects; he polished the stocks of his rifles and oiled their blue metal barrels with infinite patience. He would linger over the small, complex parts on his antique matchlock gun, making soft, caressing movements with his hands. Years later, as a new doctor, he took specialized training in hand surgery, learning to repair the small, complex bones, the exquisite neural networks, the delicate tracery of blood vessels.

When she was angry, my mother's hands were skirmishers: They could spank, slap hard, tear off clothes and scrub mightily in rage, then tug on pajamas and force the body into bed. They could force a swearing son to wash his own mouth out with soap.

Our father sometimes liked to roughhouse. I remember being lifted shrieking over his head, somersaulted out of my undershirt onto the bed and tickled to the point of hysteria, or swung around and around at the end of his arms, his two strong hands gripping my wrists, my feet not allowed to touch the ground.

Perhaps because we had no idea of using our hands for comfort, we children couldn't keep them off each other; we wrestled and fought, ambushed and attacked. In theory it was all friendly, what you'd expect in a family of big, healthy boys and a tomboy little sister. Some of it *was* friendly, and

27

gave us some feeling for our bodies. But much of it was in deadly earnest; we fought like animals over a kill, or over territory. Our mother had very little ground to give us, and we were rife with polarizations. Arno and Hal, the two older boys, stocky and dark-haired, clearly took after their father. The youngest boy, Erik, and myself, both of us blond and high-strung, clearly belonged to our mother. Erik and Hal, only two years apart, fought for the right to exist, or for dominance, or both. Erik and I, four years apart, fought purely for existence.

Erik, born prematurely, was our mother's favorite. When I was born, he wanted passionately to kill me. When I survived to be old enough to play with him, our mother expected us to play nicely, meaning quietly, so when we wrestled to the death I was not allowed to cry out. To demonstrate this, Erik once held a pillow over my face for as long as he dared. Terror ballooned in me, but when he finally let up, or I struggled free, I didn't scream or run to our mother. I had already exchanged such needs for a piece of the family wisdom: Nothing is worse than the disruption of a mother's solitude.

MY MOTHER'S aesthetic sensibility gave her some refuge from our childish imperfections. She found relief in looking out of her body onto beauty, onto color and perfection of form. Her mother, that aesthetician of the ordinary, had taught her to celebrate everyday objects, and my mother was always alive to the colors, shapes, and patterns of things. Cooking or canning or serving dinner were occasions for small pleasures: vegetables turning a vivid, intense green in boiling water; tomatoes emerging from the canning pot red jewels in the jar; orange carrots and white potatoes heaped on a dark green plate.

Sometimes she would stare at something so intensely that she seemed to project herself right into it. I remember once, as a very small child, coming up the front walk with her and realizing suddenly that she wasn't really there; she had stopped and gone into a sort of overdrive, into pure awareness of the clouds, hundreds of tiny individual floating sunsets, pale pink in the pale blue, late-afternoon Indiana sky.

She didn't turn to share her pleasure, and I thought of something, a gesture of goodness, that might compete with the clouds for her attention; I skipped ahead of her up the walk to help an even tinier child tie his shoe. I didn't score; she remained remote. Maybe she wasn't feeling pleasure at all; maybe she was just yearning toward that distant perfection. Maybe that's why her escapes were always solitary.

WHAT I remember best when I think of my mother is the house where she killed herself. We moved there right after World War II, that odd, theatrical period in which I came into consciousness of the world, my father had a very good time playing with railroads in Persia, and my mother had a difficult time cooped up with four contentious children in a little tract house on the outskirts of Fort Wayne, Indiana, a thousand miles from her natural milieu, the East Coast.

My father was a railroad man, a civil engineer. For twelve

years before the war my mother had followed him around the Pennsylvania Railroad, having babies and taking care of them, keeping house, keeping my father fed and ironed, and, whenever he was transferred, packing up everything and everyone and moving to a strange town. There she would unpack, settle my brothers into new schools, find the grocery store and dry cleaner and hardware store and liquor store, and make friends in the neighborhood, always knowing it was all temporary, that she would soon be packing up again and moving on. She didn't plant gardens, so she didn't can vegetables and she didn't make jelly. During the war, she didn't even plant a Victory Garden.

When the war was over, and my father was transferred to Philadelphia, the Pennsylvania Railroad's headquarters town, everyone seemed to assume he was there to stay. My mother, who turned forty that year, decided it was safe to commit herself. She set out to make our new house and its yard her truest expression of her chosen self.

It's still there on the Main Line, a big Victorian, one of a pair built in the 1880s by a fond father, a brewmaster for the Schmidt brewery, as wedding presents for his daughters. (The Schmidts had built a big estate nearby, and may have given him the land.) It was a perfect house for a railroad man's family, with its long acre lot nestling up against the curving arms of track that give the Main Line its name, the main line of the Pennsylvania Railroad, running west through Paoli toward Chicago.

It's a welcoming house, with high-ceilinged rooms, two fireplaces, a wide front stair and a spiral back staircase down which children can rush headlong from third floor to basement. A broad porch, suitable for lounging, eating, playing, even roller-skating, wraps around the thick gray stone walls of the first floor, so the downstairs is always cool in summer and warm in winter. The upper two floors are sheathed in pentagonal wooden shingles and have graceful arcs of wooden gingerbread set into the gable ends.

Despite these advantages, the price must have been low, because Victorian had been out of fashion since the twenties, and the house stood in a little pocket of down-at-heel period pieces in an otherwise upscale neo-Tudor and Georgian neighborhood in a residential area called St. Davids. Our house was sandwiched in between its sister house, then inhabited by a bibulous Irish justice of the peace and his family, and an empty, green-shingled gingerbread hulk with an overgrown front yard and a huge rectangular pit in the back half acre, remnant of a mushroom-farming operation that had once sprawled across all three back lots. Our house still had its elegant, gingerbread-trimmed double outhouse, although a bathroom with claw-and-ball tub and marble sink had been installed on the second floor. The furnace burned coal, and the upper stories, painted in Victorian colors, dun with brown trim, were innocent of insulation.

The recluse from whom my father bought the house had not been a tidy man; my mother hired a firm of cleaners who spent days scrubbing the interior from top to bottom. Then she decorated it. Under her direction, we all helped paint the living room a soft, pale peach that brought out the dark blue of the tiles around the corner fireplace. We painted it to last.

Despite what happened there, I still feel nostalgic for that house. Nostalgia is a treacherous emotion, cloyed with sentimentality, and I know that I long as much for the optimism of our first few years in it as for the house itself, but it was a wonderful place to live in, nonetheless. Every child had a separate bedroom, and there were still two left over for a guest room and what was then just starting to be called a family room. The kitchen was huge, there was an enclosed back porch for winter storage and summer meals, and the dining room looked exactly the way a dining room should look, with two big windows through which the sun poured in and on whose two-foot-wide sills my mother set her pans of bread dough to rise. We painted the corner-fireplace mantel dark green, with apple-green walls to set it off. My mother hung her father's paintings, and a woodcut she had made before she married my father, of city roofs and water tanks.

Outside she covered the ground with gardens. She pulled out glass and rocks and weeds and tilled in peat moss and sheep manure and water until the hard yellow clay was soft as loam. Along the porch she planted rhododendrons and azaleas, zinnias and bleeding heart. Her mother came to help; Emma, my grandmother, who could make anything grow. "Spit in the hole," my grandmother would say, and I did, onto the hose-soaked dried sheep manure mixed with dirt to cut its burning strength. Then my grandmother would hold the small bush while I troweled the soft brown earth in around it, patting so, gently, to form a mound to support the young stem. We spat in the hole for luck, for love.

My mother planted young box bushes around the edge of the semicircle of lawn inside the front carriage drive, then chased the dogs that yellowed them with urine. She put sweet william in the big quartz urn that stood in the center of the semicircle. In the shade of the maple trees that bordered the front of the property, pachysandra spread luxuriantly from her seedlings.

Her rose bushes bloomed florid pink and heavy in a sunny corner of the side yard. We children would pick off the Japanese beetles that swarmed over them, dropping them into a jar of kerosene for a nickel or dime when the jar was full.

Mint, that spreads like a weed, had its own patch at the end of the porch. Morning glories ran on strings to the porch railing, pale pink and blue translucent parachutes drifting down to the spiky green forest below. In the summer, we would pick fresh sprigs of mint for our iced tea.

Behind a high green privet hedge, the back carriage drive ran downhill to the old brick carriage house. My mother commandeered my father and a friend to clear the slope below the drive and help her build a rock garden. Below the slope, on level ground in front of the carriage house, she and my father cleared a plot and fenced it in for a vegetable garden. They embedded the chicken-wire fence a foot deep to keep out the rabbits. The whole family was pressed into service to plant chard and spinach, string beans and cabbage, carrots and cucumbers. Outside the fence, rhubarb flourished, and in summer the asparagus bed, gone to seed, grew into a cloud of long, pale, feathery fronds.

In spring and summer there were planting and weeding and eating. All summer and into the fall my mother canned and made great batches of jelly, dripping red from its cloth bag hung in the corner. She stacked the big glass Mason jars of tomatoes and peaches and peas and beans on rough plank shelves in the basement.

On summer evenings I loved to go down to the garden to pick fresh chard for supper, squatting in the dark, soft earth, surrounded by the mysterious presence of growing vegetables, alive but silent, seeming to rustle as tiny bugs moved through their kingdom.

Even weeding could be a satisfaction; the sharp tug at the offending plant, the soft giving-way of the roots in the well-cultivated earth, the quick toss onto the heap of yellowing greens at the edge of the bed. When a bed was clean, my mother or father would add the weeds to the hot, rich, mysterious stew of the compost heap.

In the kitchen, my mother ruled, and I was her apprentice. She made the bread dough; I kneaded to the limit of my seven-year-old strength. She put together the ingredients for cake batter; I mixed with the big wooden spoon, stirring until the dark chocolate stream marbled, spread, and blended with the pale flour and milk. Together, Erik and I prepared the margarine: One of us would tear open the corner of the small packet of food coloring, sprinkling or pouring it over the dead-white lump of vegetable paste. The other would mix, slowly pulling the iridescent orange coloring into streaks and puddles of yellow, growing paler and paler as it merged with the white until it was all pale yellow.

We molded the mess into a rough lump and set it in the refrigerator to harden.

My mother presided over rituals of transformation: Small hard seeds sprouted into plants, the slick dough emerged as hot bread, the stirred batter became the risen cake. Kitchen-magic was her specialty; to a child, she guaranteed every day the rebirth of the world.

FOUR

Cunning
Little Compartments:
A Portrait of My Father
and His Railroad

M Y FATHER brought home some K-rations after the war, although it's certain he never had to eat any. They were a curiosity, kept in a cabinet in the old butler's pantry in St. Davids. When I discovered them one day, we were allowed to open and examine them, several years old as they must have been. I loved the many little containers of heavily waxed cardboard or tin. My father's life was full of cunning little compartments: sleeping cars on trains, his desk drawers, his cabinet of antique drafting tools, the pockets of his suit and vest. When his little compartments were comfortably filled, he would smile around his pipe.

The rosewood drawers of his shaving mirror were full of old coins, miniature army patches, an old wallet or two, a packet of condoms. Little boxes full of odd studs and cuff links. The drawers had an odor at once richly pungent and musty—a man's mystery. They smelled of old leather, hand oil, ancient flakes of pipe tobacco. My father's was a mystery of small dark boxes.

HE SHARED a walk-through closet with my mother. Her clothes were on their bedroom side; his side opened from the big room we used as a family room—a combination den, playroom, and extra guest room. When you opened up the door on my mother's side of the closet, you could see my father's dark wool suits looming behind her tweeds.

He kept his shoes in neat rows on the floor, each pair with its wooden shoe-trees. He believed in taking good care of shoes, as of all objects, and he instructed me carefully on how to polish mine. He taught me to put newspapers on the floor, to wash my oxfords first with water, to put the polish on with a brush and let it dry before rubbing up a shine with a clean, soft cloth. I would get polish all over my hands and clothes as well as the newspapers and the floor. My father was scornful of my efforts, but I really believed that if I polished my shoes well enough, and neatly enough, I could share in the golden glow of approval that he reserved for objects properly cared for. He praised his ten-year-old English shoes, his twenty-year-old custom-made suits. He yearned for the batman who had brushed his uniforms during the war; he expected his wife to brush his suit and topcoat before he left the house, and to brush his suit again before she hung it in the closet.

He was not a tall man; only five-feet-nine or so, with the heavy bones and solid, chunky build of his German ancestors. By the time I was nine or ten I could reach his cheek with my lips if I stood on tiptoe. He would permit a kiss when he came home from work, turning his head slightly and holding his cheek out toward me the way his mother always did. She never allowed anyone to kiss her on the lips; she thought it was unsanitary. Her skin was soft and smelled faintly of lavender water; my father's skin, stubbly with beard in the evening, smelled of aftershave. He had a red patch, a birthmark, on the back of his neck, partly hidden by the neat line of stubble created by his barber's clippers. He had thick, almost blue-black hair that he wore short on the sides and long on top.

He fancied himself a tough, hard-bitten type, like the railroad section men he had idolized as a boy, who bossed the track crews in whipcord breeches and leather boots, chewing tobacco and spitting it accurately between the sleepers. But my father was something of a dandy and liked to indulge his taste for civilized pleasures. He kept his Havana cigars in a cork-lined wooden humidor on the sideboard, above the shelves stocked with liqueurs: Strega, Chartreuse, Cherry Heering, Benedictine & Brandy, Drambuie, Kirschwasser.

These were the domestic accoutrements of a gentleman. My father was not really a drinking man, but he considered it part of the essential equipment of manhood to be able to hold your liquor. During the war, when his troops had run supply trains north through Persia from Teheran to the Russian border, he had survived many nights of head-to-head toasting over dinner with his Russian counterparts. The only war story he ever told was about those evenings.

The toasts were in straight vodka; the object was to be the last man on his feet. My father brought home a medal from the Russians that he had earned, he always claimed, by outdrinking so many of their officers.

Serious drinking required serious preparation. As my three brothers became old enough to drink, my father passed his methods on to them: at dinner, you drink milk and eat mashed potatoes, preferably with gravy. These line your stomach so that it takes a long time for the liquor to soak through into your system. One reason the Russians could hold their vodka so well was that their diet consisted largely of potatoes, meat, and gravy. The milk was an American touch.

My father did not pass this lore on to me; I was a girl. But he was liberal about alcohol at home. As we children reached the age of ten or so we were allowed a drop of liqueur after dinner, just to acquire a taste for it; as teenagers we could have a cocktail before dinner if we wanted one. His philosophy was that if we learned to handle alcohol at home, we wouldn't have problems with it later. At quite an early age I liked an old fashioned before dinner and a B & B or Drambuie after. My father never stopped trying to get me to drink Strega, though; perhaps he thought the cloyingly sweet chartreuse liqueur was more suitable for a girl.

It was a time when men wore hats; my father bought his from J. Press in Philadelphia. In summer he always wore a handmade panama; in winter a felt fedora that went with his suit or topcoat. His winter suits were English wool; his summer suits finely spun, lightweight wool, linen, or seersucker — until drip-dry fabrics appeared. He fell in love with those. He loved washing out the nearly transparent white shirts, through which, when he had his coat off, you could clearly see the outline of his T-shirt. Except in the hottest weather he always wore a vest, to hold a watch chain with a Pennsylvania Railroad keystone hanging from it.

He had set his heart early on the Pennsy, the glory of the East, its Twentieth Century Limited steaming straight out the Main Line from Philadelphia, across the length of Pennsylvania to the Allegheny Mountains, almost touching its tail as it rounded the Horseshoe Curve to Pittsburgh, then running flat out to Chicago, gateway to the West.

Inside there were brass fittings in the compartments and white linen tablecloths in the dining car. My father came to know the steward personally, as eventually he knew practically every conductor, Pullman porter, engineer, and brakeman on the line. When we rode the train overnight, my father would disappear into the men's room lounge, with its leather couches and club chairs only partially concealed behind a green leather curtain, to talk railroading, tell stories, smoke and — who knew? — play cards all night with the conductor and the porter. As a civil engineer, my father was both an aristocrat in the great society of men who could work with their hands and a brother in the fraternity of railroad men.

When he met my mother, he was still only a baby tough guy. In his college photos, even in his ROTC uniform, with stiff-collared tunic, puttees and a flat-brimmed ranger hat, he is chubby-cheeked and his mouth looks sensitive. He looks like a boy who could send his fiancée art books and tell her how much he missed her. (I know he did this, because when I was fifteen I read their letters, tucked away upstairs in a dresser drawer, saved relentlessly through her suicide and his remarriage. He kept his army uniforms, too, down in the basement in a trunk.)

He studied civil engineering under his own father, who was head of the engineering department at Gettysburg College. When my father graduated, the Pennsy didn't have any openings, so he got a job as stake boy on a surveying crew for the Louisville & Nashville Railroad. In his hightop shoes, puttees, and breeches, he hiked into the backwoods from Bristol, on the Tennessee/Virginia state line. (When his family wrote to him, they put both states on the envelope.) In a year or so, he was drawing the maps and someone else was carrying the stakes. But then he was bitten by a copperhead, and one of the crew cored the flesh around the bite right out of his leg. That was enough for my father; he quit and came home to Gettysburg.

He was still set on the Pennsy, but they still didn't have an opening. In the meantime, his mother's friend Elsie Singmaster, the writer, needed a chauffeur. She had a new Packard sedan, but she certainly wasn't going to learn to drive. My father had been driving since he was thirteen, which was when Sara, his mother, had bought her first car. Elsie Singmaster had known my father all his life, so she hired him to drive her around the southern Pennsylvania countryside as far as Harrisburg, where she could look at the Susquehanna River, which ran through most of her novels. They took a trip south, to Virginia and the Carolinas. My father sat up on the leather front seat of the Packard in his

SIGNE HAMMER

plus-fours and cap, a lot happier and cleaner than he had
been as a surveyor in Tennessee/Virginia.

When he finally got his first maintenance-of-way job on
the Pennsylvania Railroad it was right on the tracks, just like
the section men of his boyhood. Soon after he married my
mother, he was managing a freight branch on Delaware's
Eastern Shore; over the years, he worked his way up to run
whole divisions, with the stations and freight yards their
nerve centers: Harrisburg, Pennsylvania, and Indianapolis,
Indiana (where I was born in 1940), and, right before the
war, a big one, Washington Terminal in Washington, D.C.
When he returned from the war, he was sent back East to
run the Pennsy's headquarters division from an office in
Philadelphia's Thirtieth Street Station, a neoclassical monument to the great age of railroading. He had come out of the
war a colonel, and remained one in the Army Reserve; he
seemed to be well on his way to both his life's ambitions — to
become a general of the Army and a vice president of the
Pennsylvania Railroad. (In those days, vice presidencies
weren't routinely given out to up-and-coming young man-
agers; there were generally very few in a company, and the
title was a fitting cap to a successful career.)

Even when he ascended to offices, my father never lost his
love of the solid, sulfurous, steel-and-wood glory of the
trains. When I was a little girl, the romance of the railroads
clung to him. On the Main Line, we children would run
down to the back yard to see a steam engine go by, hauling
an endless chain of freight cars carrying the names, initials,
or insignia of the Nickel Plate, C & N, B & O, Wabash, and
twenty other lines long since consigned to oblivion. Rail-

42

roads went places, and I was a child who loved to roam away from home. I could identify the provenance of railroad freight cars the way other kids could identify Fords and Chevies. I felt a profound identification with my father's love of his work, his joyful swagger when he showed us around a station or introduced us to one of his cronies on the caboose.

I remember waking up in the lower bunk of a sleeping car on a train stopped somewhere in the middle of the night, raising the blind, and seeing a pair of blue-overalled legs stride by, a lantern swinging alongside them, and thinking, My father knows that man. I thought all the railroad men I saw or met—big, burly, genial, cigar- or cigarette-smoking men, except for dining-car stewards, who were slim and dapper and genial—were my friends and protectors.

I didn't know what a vice presidency, a mere abstraction, was. I thought my father had ascended to something like heaven when he ran Pennsylvania Station in New York, the jewel of the system, a great crystal palace with blue smoke drifting high up under the glass, and the fabulous echoes of the announcer's voice over the microphone: "Now departing, on Tee-rack Num-ber Si-ix, the Bu-rawd-way Limited! Newark, Tren-ton, North Philadelphee-yay, Thirtieth Street Staa-tion, Pee-o-li, Altoona, Pitts-burgh, Chicago! All-l-l abo-awd!"

FIVE

Norwegian Wood

ABOUT THE time my father joined the surveying crew in Tennessee/Virginia, my mother, Agnes, was a freshman at Barnard College in New York, studying Chaucer and art and history. She was a quiet, thoughtful, nervous girl, a craftsperson like her mother and father. She was bookish but not scholarly, and she lived at home with her parents in Douglaston, Long Island, where she had grown up learning to use her father's paints and carving tools and her mother's clay and kiln. As a small child she had been a little mouse in her father's studio, watching him work, watching his face change with the light and the task. Trygve had a hawk nose and a slash of mouth set to patience as he shaped the clay into the image of the live hawk chained to a perch across the studio. He was engrossed; my mother could stay there and play with her scrap of clay as long as she didn't make any sudden sound or move quickly and disturb the hawk, who stared at her father with the same fierce concentration her father gave to the clay.

Her mother, Emma, taught her to pot. My mother learned well; she gave her future mother-in-law (the one who would forbid divorce), a finely glazed, apple-green bowl, wheel-turned, shaped at the top into four rounded corners—a bowl for fruit to ripen in on a table under a sunny window. When my grandmother died, she left it to me. It sits on the table in my small apartment, under the window. Sometimes I put fruit in it, but more often I toss in odds and ends: a couple of ballpoint pens, some 35 mm slides, a rubber band, a clothespin, a few packets of Moist Towelettes. Things that disguise the bowl, make it look ordinary. But it's still her bowl.

My mother learned printmaking from Trygve. In 1927, after she left Barnard and three years before she married my father, she made the woodcut that later, in Pennsylvania, she hung in our dining room. Now it hangs in my apartment, in Manhattan where it belongs; it's a classic New York skyline, rooftops and water tanks, flattened to planes and angles and shallow curves—a vision informed by precisionism, Sheeler's and Demuth's American take on cubism. Only it's done in crayon colors: a red water tank with a green roof, a blue stovepipe with a little tin hat, building walls shading from crisp red-orange to burning yellow. The mood is cheerful; she was having a good time in her father's studio, making art.

As a child, I sometimes made things with my mother. Once during the war, when I was very small and we were living in Indiana, my mother found a clay bluff she thought would serve. We drove out there and she and my oldest brother dug spadefuls of clay from the bottom of the bluff, and we took it home in a carton. Freed of domestic formalities by my father's absence, my mother planned to get a wheel and do some real potting, but in the meantime she made small animals with us children, or at least with me. My animals had pinched ears and stubby, uncertain legs. My mother baked them, unglazed, under coals in the fireplace; they came out scorched around the ears and feet, but they were genuine little terra-cotta creatures.

Freshman year was all my mother had at Barnard. My aunt and uncle maintained that she had to quit and get a job because by the mid-twenties the Depression was already starting for a lot of people.

Trygve and Emma both taught; he, sculpture and wood-carving to professional students in Manhattan; she, pottery to the wives and daughters of middle-class Douglaston. She kept all the records and made sure the bills got paid. He became well known as a decorative artist, and he designed everything from book jackets to Princeton University's athletic trophy room and various memorials, war and otherwise. He carved and painted polychrome wood screens for the altars of churches, sculpted busts of Norwegian heroes like Amundson and Ibsen, and painted murals in hotels and restaurants. A lot of commercial work came through Rambusch, a big decorating firm in Greenwich Village: elaborate woodcarving for the Norse Grill in the Waldorf Astoria, and sculpting handsome animal and bird figures in bronze or stone for the gateposts of the estates of the nouveaux riches in Southampton. And all the time he was exhibiting his own sculpture. He was, in short, artist and craftsman both, unfussy about distinctions between the two. As a young man he had absorbed the ideals of William Morris's Arts and Crafts Movement, and he worked in a period in which design achieved, nearly, the status of high art.

For years he and my grandmother managed pretty well; they built a house, rented summer cottages, sent my mother to a private school and to Barnard. And then something happened. Maybe it was purely a matter of money. You would think there would have been plenty of work at the height of the twenties, but perhaps there finally weren't enough commissions, and not enough money from teaching. Or my grandfather was spending too much. Or maybe my grandparents just didn't think college was all that important for a girl; they both came from Norway, where, much as in any other country, boys were favored and girls took their chances.

After she left college, my mother got a job as a legal secretary. For the next five years, until she decided to marry my father, she spent her days typing out briefs for lawyers. She gave her parents most of her salary and went on living at home, spending as much time as she could in the studio. If she was disappointed, she didn't show it. She was used to helping out. She had learned early that her mother's priorities were Trygve, her house, her gardens, her cooking, her pottery. Trygve's were himself, his work, and Emma. My mother and her brother were part of the household; the Norwegian family was not what you would call child-centered.

Trygve and Emma had come a long way together. My grandfather was born into a large, well-to-do merchant family in Arendal, a port town on the sheltered southeast coast below Christiana, as Oslo, the Norwegian capital, was called then. After six hundred years of control first by the Danes and then by the Swedes, nineteenth-century Norway was a tight, self-righteous, Lutheran country, with a streak of crudeness running alongside a wide vein of hard labor. Its great playwright Ibsen, unable to earn a living in what little theater there was, had exiled himself to Europe, where he wrote plays about Norway that deeply offended his countrymen. He didn't come back until he was so famous even the Norwegians couldn't spit on him. An aging celebrity with an eye for young girls, he held court at his table in the Grand Café in Christiana. He was still alive, felled by strokes but a great symbol of integrity, when my grandparents sailed off to their own artistic exile.

Trygve's grandfather, the son of a policeman, had married a wealthy shipowner's daughter, giving him access to the means to make his own fortune in trade. He sent goods-laden ships across the Skagerak to Denmark and down the coast to Germany and France and England, the captains keeping careful notations of their selling and buying in little books covered with marble paper and leather. His son Joseph, Trygve's uncle, also had sound mercantile instincts; he opened a big hardware store in Arendal. But Joseph's younger brother, Christopher Natvig, Trygve's father and my great-grandfather, was different. The family had sent him to England for an education, and he had returned a dandy and *litterateur,* who could not or would not bother to make a go of the grocery store with which his father set him up. His behavior was a local scandal. When I was a teenager I met some ancient relations who were still indignant about the way my great-grandfather would lie on the couch reading poetry while his wife made Christmas for their seven children.

My great-grandmother was a consul's daughter from Flekkefjord, a port town on the stormy southwest coast. Christopher Natvig's parents had no doubt hoped she would shape up their son, but he passed on to his children his un-Norwegian proclivities, including a taste for life outside the stuffy society of Arendal. It was a time when, all over Europe, where the cultures of peasantry, bourgeoisie, and aristocracy seemed frozen together in a century that was finished, people were leaving cities, towns, villages, farms, and ghettos and sailing to America to reinvent themselves. One of Trygve's older brothers, Rolf, became an opera singer, married an actress, and settled over here. Trygve turned down a job as clerk in his uncle's hardware store to head across the ocean in 1902, at twenty-four.

He met Emma on the boat. She was twenty. "It was what you did," she told me years later, when I asked her about setting off for America by herself. Both her brothers had already gone. She was a tiny, elfin, round-faced girl with snapping round eyes and a small pointed nose. She was somehow both homely and pretty, perhaps because she was part Lapp. Her family had come from up north, near

Trondheim, to a farm in the south. I don't know whether it was like one of the old hill farms I've seen, a little compound of buildings huddled together, house by barn by shed. In winter, on such farms, daughters slept above the cow barn for warmth, while sons slept in the house loft above the stove. In summer, though, the girls had their own loft above the hay barn, airy and sweet-smelling and free.

Nor do I know when my grandmother went to Christiana—whether she went to go to school or get a job or just to get on the boat. She always claimed that she got there early enough to be bought a glass of wine by Ibsen in the Grand Café, she and a little group of friends who were not afraid to flirt with him. But she missed the torchlight parade the women of Christiana held to honor the returning author of *The Doll's House.* From his balcony at the Grand Hotel, above the café, Ibsen had told them to go home and take care of their husbands.

But women were leaving the country as eagerly as men. In 1898 Trygve's eighteen-year-old sister Signe, my great-aunt, for whom I was named, was the first of the family to go to America. Another sister, Ebba, went as far as Christiana, where she ran a boardinghouse for gentlemen of the *Storting,* the Norwegian parliament.

My mother did not inherit this passion for leaving. She was more like my great-aunt Töna, another of Trygve's sisters, who stayed home in Arendal to keep house for her father after their mother died. It was not uncommon in the nineteenth century for one daughter to be sacrificed, or to sacrifice herself, in this way—Emma's younger sister stayed home, too. Töna taught basket weaving and other genteel crafts to the proper daughters of Arendal until her father died, and then she moved in with Ebba in Christiana and helped her keep the boardinghouse.

In her whole life, my mother never struck out on her own, either; unless, of course, you count her suicide. To set out voluntarily for death must count for something in the way of courage. You might also count her getting married; as Colette wrote, there was no bravery like that of a young woman who married and went alone to live in the house of a strange man.

Her own mother hadn't had to do that, exactly; my grandmother and grandfather built their house together in a strange land. In Norway Trygve had grown up in a big square white clapboard house that would have suited Nantucket or Martha's Vineyard, but in Douglaston he and Emma built a traditional Norwegian house, carved inside and out with folk motifs. Even the beam ends were carved, and the red shutters. They built slowly, room by room, as they had the money—starting, of course, with the studio, where at first, my mother and her little brother took their baths in the art tub, otherwise used to keep clay wet and to wash brushes.

They were house proud. Trygve, of course, did all the decorative woodcarving. Emma covered the grounds with gardens, while in the copper-roofed studio Trygve drew and painted the house in a sunny, impressionistic style. In our dining room in St. Davids my mother hung a pastel of the high gable end of her parents' house, morning glories trailing from its second-floor window box. My grandmother kept an oil of the big front hall, its coatrack covered with her and my grandfather's famous, fantastic assortment of hats.

In the summers, like all good Norwegians, my grandparents would take a cottage at a lake or beach in the midst of a whole colony of friends, with whom they would eat outdoors at long trestle tables under the trees, with bottles of wine and much joshing. Larking for a snapshot, the family lined up in a row, belly to back, largest to smallest, on the porch of one summer's beach cottage. My grandfather's paunch, in a striped wool tank top that overhangs his knee-length wool trunks, just touches his wife's shoulder blades, encased in a puffed-sleeve bathing dress. She wears a frilled cap. My mother, about twelve, and my uncle Olaf, four, wear long wool tank tops and tight, knee-length trunks like their father's.

It was a family in which looking was important; looking at the things you painted or drew, looking at the clay as you modeled it with the fine, smooth, wooden tools that turn so sensuously in the hand. Emma and Trygve looked at their children and took pictures that show what they saw: my mother, solemn-faced, in a white cotton dress with a square yoke neck, her long blond hair secured by a wide ribbon with a bow on top, standing next to her little brother Olaf. Perched on a chair, he wears tights and a tunic hand-knit by Emma. His blond hair is cropped in a Dutch-boy bob; he looks angelic. My mother's eyes are big, soft, and guarded. Her mouth is soft, too, but firmly set. Posing is natural to her; she has long since learned patience, and waiting, and reticence.

As a Norwegian man and an artist, my grandfather naturally womanized. He flirted with his daughter's friends when they became old enough to look like women, and he slept with the wives of the friends he and Emma summered with, or with women he met in the Village when he went in to see Rambusch.

Emma must have known about this, but she was stoic by temperament, and in Europe, where her outlook had been formed, affairs were a man's prerogative. If she felt betrayed, or angry, or sad, she didn't show it. She believed you could shape your life, beautifully, the way you shaped objects, creating harmony in relationships and in the ordering of your days. Rather than confront her husband, she would retreat into her own fastnesses. She could sit still for a long time in peaceful meditation, a small, serene smile on her face. She could lose herself in creating her beautiful objects.

But not completely. It was understood that, while Emma and Trygve both practiced their crafts for love and money, art was for love alone and therefore finer. As an artist, and a man, Trygve was considered finer than Emma, and therefore unsuited to dealing with worldly things; while Emma, as a craftsperson and a woman, was eminently suited to dealing with exactly those things.

She was a strong wife, by the American standards of her day, because she earned money, but in her own Norwegian farm tradition women could work as hard as men, and earn money from chickens and eggs, without being equal, without ever challenging the men. Like any other wife, Emma made sure her husband ate well and was not distracted by petty details. Trygve could make any decisions he liked, and she would follow; if he was feckless about money it wasn't her role to reign him in. Still, she had dedicated her life to taking care of him, and that meant protecting him as much as possible from his own folly. The advantage of her situation, the source of her power as a wife, was that she knew she was essential to him.

They probably had to take out a mortgage, and there were school bills, and Trygve must have spent a certain amount on women. It probably didn't take much to tip the balance to red. My mother's leaving school was only the beginning; when, in the early thirties, the time came, Emma, the worldly one, sold the house and found an apartment.

EMMA WAS a good mother, after her own views. On the farm, children had grown up a little like animals; they were expected to do their chores and work hard, but there had been a servant girl and a hired man, so there was time and freedom for dreaming. As for what they thought and felt, they were left pretty much alone, except for Lutheran services on Sundays. When Olaf was born it was natural that Emma should give her eight-year-old daughter a lot of his care. On farms, the smaller children were always the responsibility of the older girls. Emma and Trygve both had to be free to do their work, and Olaf had no interest in art. Once he smashed a plaster model with a hammer, just to see what would happen.

Agnes was wonderfully responsible and inventive about caring for her little brother. She taught him to read by reading to him and showing him the letters and the words. She made up little games to distract him; in one, the first to find the most letters of the alphabet on a specific page of a book won. (Later, she played this game and a variant, hunt-

ing for letters on roadside signs from the car, with my
brothers; later still, she persuaded my brothers to play the
car version with me, as a way of teaching me to read and
keeping us all distracted.)

She fit in easily with her parents' aesthetic ideals and with
their politics, which were a kind of aesthetic socialism. She
could work demon-hard, as Norwegians can, and she was
full of ideals herself, about purity of motive and her responsibility to help create harmony in the family.

But she was perpetually on the outside. Despite her
father's philandering, he and her mother were solid, a
unit—as if, having left their country, they had substituted
each other, right or wrong. Nor could my mother really
share her mother's unflappable calmness, her iron-clad serenity. If Emma dealt with the uncomfortable or the unpleasant by retreating into an aesthetic and quasi-religious
space of her own (she was always taking up some mystical
or philosophical movement, from theosophy to Unity),
my mother—who certainly carried with her the turmoil,
the disturbing weakness, the unpredictability of body and
feelings common to infants and small children—must
frequently have been the occasion for her mother's
withdrawal.

Emma's ability to distance herself bound Trygve to her.
He believed her to be a manifestation of the eternal femi-
nine, carrying within herself the bottomless reserves of
acceptance and forgiveness every man dreams of. But to my
mother, who desperately needed a response, Emma's retreats must have been devastating. My grandmother could
garden as a way of smoothing, taming, controlling the

world, and Agnes could work peacefully next to her. Emma could cook, and can, and bake, and so make kitchen-magic, and pass on her skills to her daughter. But when she went into one of her impregnable retreats, she left my mother with nothing.

My grandmother once confided in me that my mother had been an anxious person, that she didn't seem to have much confidence in herself, intimating that that alone may have been why she dropped out of college. Perhaps it was. Yet she was a success before college, at Drew Seminary for young ladies. She had a tight group of girlfriends; in the summers they would picnic together, posing for photographs leaning against a plank fence or on a flat rock in a stream. In those pictures, they look smart and unhurried, like people who have time to plan their lives. They were fourteen when women got the vote; they absorbed the heady feminism that followed World War I. They read poetry by Edna St. Vincent Millay and Sara Teasdale, and believed in the future of women.

When I knew her, my mother was both anxious and a ferocious perfectionist, but I never made a connection between the two, never considered that the perfectionism might be an antidote to poisonous anxiety. Barnard was tougher and more competitive than prep school, full of fiercely intelligent young women eager to excel. Maybe it seemed too hard to compete with them, so that dropping out, prolonging her girlhood, was a relief. By the look of the art my mother made, she was happy enough living at home, working at a job that was exacting and demanded some intelligence but not a lot of initiative. She spent five years among lawyers without marrying one of them, so she doesn't seem to have been in a great hurry to move on.

There is no evidence that she ever considered making woodcuts or pottery to sell, or teaching other people to make them, or both. Perhaps that was because her mother's and father's arts and crafts had failed her. Or perhaps her proper girls' seminary—or her parents, reverting to the values of their own families—had encouraged her to think of herself as a well-brought-up young lady for whom potting and printmaking were pleasant accomplishments, but who would not, should not, ever have to earn her living by them.

Or maybe it was just that no one had bothered to encourage her. Her parents saw that she was shy, and nervous, and unsure of herself, but if someone had told them that she needed special support, more encouragement, they would have been astonished. They had found their own ways out of the constraints not only of their families but of their entire culture—why should they expect anything less of their daughter? Besides, it was a different time, a different place. At the turn of the century Norway had been a place you left, America a place you went to. My mother was born in America; it was for her to grow up American, marry an American, and live the American dream.

Which was what she wanted, too, at least by the time she met my father. She seems never to have considered, say, heading for Greenwich Village to set up in a studio and embark on the life of privation a young artist or craftsperson faced. Of course, the Village was her father's territory.

Rambusch was there, his cafés were there, his women werethere. How could my mother have created herself on his turf?

In any case, she was tired of bohemian insecurity, so of the possibilities offered by her mother's life she chose those of the conventional wife: house, garden, kitchen, and children. When the time came to grow up and leave home she was ready to turn away from her crafts even as a hobby. She never took her crafts or her art into her own hands, never tried to make them her life, and when she took her fate into her own hands she had completely abandoned the art that might have given her a reason, the craft that might have enabled her to live.

SIX

German-American Relations

MY PARENTS were married in June 1930, in Trygve
and Emma's garden in Douglaston. He was twenty-
six; she was twenty-four. In the black-and-white photographs, they look small and slim and homely. His mouth is
very wide. Her dress is a long, loose white wrap with a long
lace veil draped over her head like a mantilla. The jacket of
his dark suit looks a little snug; is he already beginning to
put on weight?

She believes she has found security. She has only known
him for a few months, but he has been writing her sensitive-
sounding letters, telling her he thinks about her sitting at
her potter's wheel in the studio. When he visits, he brings
her fine, expensive art books, published in Europe, with
color plates. He is demonstrating his solvency.

They were introduced by two matchmakers: his mother

Sara's friend Elsie Singmaster, whom my father had chauffeured back in 1925 and 26, and Emma and Trygve's neighbor Althea Knickerbocker. Althea and Elsie were old friends, and when Althea heard about John she said he simply had to meet Agnes. Late in 1929 she took my mother down to Gettysburg, and Elsie Singmaster took them both over to visit her old friend Sara, whose oldest son happened to be home.

My parents were both ready for marriage. My father had finally gotten a job with the Pennsylvania Railroad, and for the moment he had an apartment in Philadelphia. He went home often to visit his mother; it was easy for him to hop a train to Gettysburg and he was a good boy, a dutiful son.

My mother wanted a place in the world, some status. For a woman in those days, wife-and-mother was the approved choice. She would be recognized as an adult, be able to act in the world. She would have a daughter, who would finish college. She wanted a man with a regular salary, a man both frugal and faithful. My father, with his railroad job and his ambitions, his probity and his good family, must have looked like a terrific bet.

At the end of her visit to Gettysburg she went back to Douglaston. On weekends my father took the train up to visit her. He took her to dinner, to movies, to plays. She took him to art galleries, and he listened while, over tea, over dinner, she talked to him about art, about the things she loved to make and to look at. She assumed, naturally, that her aesthetic sensibility would shape the life she would make with him. She thought my father shared her views and approved of her style; there were his letters, and the art books he gave her, and his family. His father, Frank, was a cultivated man who taught art as well as engineering at Gettysburg College, and the gracious brick house on the outskirts of Gettysburg was furnished with fine antiques.

But they were all trade goods, so to speak. Sara ran her house as an antiques business, buying and selling the Wedgwood china and Chippendale couches. She had excellent taste, and she liked having beautiful things around her, but she would sell her living-room couch for a good price. She was well-known in the area for her sharp eye, sharper wits, and fine goods.

My grandfather Frank, on the other hand, cared very little about money. He was a scholar and a dreamer, the proverbial absentminded professor. Sara didn't care any more about his interest in art than she did for his business advice—of which she once said that she made it a rule always to do the exact opposite.

When she met Frank, he was a brilliant, precocious, twenty-two-year-old dandy, fresh from Johns Hopkins with a Ph.D. in astrophysics. For some reason he had decided not to pursue that subject as a career. Perhaps there simply weren't many job openings in what was, in 1898, still an extremely esoteric field. Or perhaps he was overcome by the family tradition of practicality. His father, a Lutheran minister, was a vigorous political man who had founded and run a college and presided over the Pennsylvania Lutheran Synod. Frank was the oldest of four sons; his father may have tolerated, even encouraged academic brilliance, but he would certainly have frowned on an impractical career. Whether or not my grandfather was divided about his choice, he seems to have given up on astrophysics immediately; he went instead to Carthage, Illinois, to teach mathematics at Carthage College for Women. There Sara Baker met him and decided to marry him.

She may have mistaken his academic achievements for ambition, but he was in no hurry. He disliked teaching women, so he moved on to take a degree in civil engineering. In those days, my uncle has pointed out, the interesting engineering was in railroad bridges. I don't know whether my grandfather regretted trading the esoteric beauty of physics for the more down-to-earth beauty—and power—of steel structures, but he began, in his way, to live the life of a practical man. He went to work for the American Bridge Company in Chicago, and finally, in 1903, he married Sara Baker. She reminded him of his mother.

His family, too, was hard on women, the Germanic tradition being not far removed from the Scandinavian in that respect. The men in the family cared mostly about their own work, and not much about people, even their own children. They went their own way and expected their women to follow, but a strong wife could do as she pleased. When Sara married Frank, his mother told her that if she wanted to have any life at all she would have to make it for herself, because Frank wouldn't give her any help.

Red-haired Sara had been a late baby, doted on by her middle-aged parents and her grandfather, and was used to doing what she wanted. She came from a family of strong and determined individuals who had arrived in America before the Revolution; some of them had pioneered in Illinois among Native Americans, and Sara's grandmother had been on friendly terms with at least two well-known chiefs. Her grandfather, Archibald Dorothy, a cattle dealer, had made his living buying longhorns driven up the Chisholm Trail from Texas to the Kansas railhead. He would drive them up through Missouri and swim them across the Mississippi River to Carthage for resale; he died, at seventy-nine, of a chill caught while crossing in midwinter.

Sara took her mother-in-law's advice. When Frank began designing steel bridges for his uncle in Chambersburg, Pennsylvania, Sara apprenticed herself to a local antiques dealer. He taught her appraising, and when her husband went to work for Bethlehem Steel in 1915, she opened her first shop. She established her independence the only way it was ever recognized in my family—financially. As my aunt said, Sara made her own decisions.

She grew to have a certain amount of contempt for her husband's disinterest in worldly things, and she raised her sons to be intensely practical. She expected a lot from them. My father was fourteen when the family moved from Bethlehem to Gettysburg. He had already started a summer job as a courier at the Bethlehem Steel mill, riding his bike the length of the miles-long sheds along the Lehigh River, past the huge open hearths spewing cherry-red rivers of molten metal, past the sweating Poles and Irishmen, who cursed good-humoredly or laughed, waving him on with his messages for the foremen down the line. It was glorious, hardly work at all.

It made no sense for a boy to give up a good summer job just because his family was moving away. My grandmother decreed that my father must stay on in Bethlehem until fall, and he moved into a boardinghouse for the rest of the summer. He thought he was proud to be on his own, like a man, but he didn't have a man's resources, and his evenings were lonely: he could go to the library or read in his room. He joined the YMCA and went to self-improvement lectures. Sometimes he swam in the pool, but his days on the bike left him without much zest for further exertion. He tried every church in town, except for the Roman Catholic, and decided he liked the Methodist best, even though he'd been christened a Lutheran. He spoke to the minister after church and made a very good impression; he was invited to Sunday dinner.

Later it was clear that my father felt deprived by that summer. He would talk about it in a way that made it sound apocalyptic, almost mythical: the time when he had had to leave home at fourteen to live and work by himself in a strange town. It became the paradigm, to which he returned again and again, of his hard life. "I couldn't just do whatever I wanted to," he'd say, angry over what he regarded as my soft and privileged life, my demanding female nature. "I've always had to work hard for a living."

Money activated his grievance. He equated its possession with having enough stuff—power, being, maybe potency—for himself. Demands for money, or the spending of his money by other people, especially women, seemed to him to be attempts to deprive him of his essential being.

When I was a freshman in college, I bought a box of stationery, an imitation parchment bond with the college seal embossed on it. It wasn't expensive—a dollar, I think, which would be perhaps eight dollars today. I wrote my first letter home on this stationery, proud to be at a good college, wanting to make a good impression.

I received one of my father's typewritten letters in return, full of bitter recriminations against me for wasting his money on good stationery when I could as easily have used a cheap yellow pad. He had worked hard for his money; it was time I learned the value of a dollar and stopped wasting my allowance on useless extravagances. Of course, he had typed this letter on stationery printed with his own name and address.

Was this chintziness merely a family trait, or foible? There is the story of my grandmother Sara and her mother-in-law, Liberty Hollinger, the one who advised her to make her own life. Once when Sara and her younger son, my uncle, were visiting for a few days, Liberty came upon Sara washing out a pair of her small son's socks. "Stop wasting my soap," Liberty peremptorily told her. Sara packed up her son and left.

Times were harder then, it's true, and there were far fewer objects around, so it was possible, perhaps even normal, to become possessive about something as elemental as a cake of soap. I can remember Sara herself, as an old woman, saving worn-down slivers of soap to put into a little wire-mesh cage with a handle. When you wanted to wash the dishes, you shook the cage around in a tin dishpan of hot water.

It's also true that my father came from a family and a time when such subjects as love were not discussed, and personal feelings were almost wholly unacknowledged. What counted was how you behaved, and that involved an intricate code of taboos and restrictions, enforced by a constant stream of dictums. My father passed these, many of them classics of everyday American Protestant social philosophy, on to us:

"Never start a sentence with 'I,' especially in a letter."

"Your name should be in the papers only three times: when you're born, when you marry, and when you die."

For years I struggled with the first commandment; I never could figure out how it was possible to obey it without resorting to corporate indirection, as in "it has been noted that," an appalling locution of the sort my father did, in fact, use. The beauty of such verbal contortions, for him as for corporations and governments, was and is that they carry authority without responsibility; no actual *person* has noticed whatever it is, just some impersonal, presumably omniscient and omnipotent Voice. The real purpose of this voice is to inspire dread, and in this, with me at least, my father succeeded.

There are other, more sinister meanings in the commandment: If you can't start a sentence with "I," you can never put yourself first. This is handy advice for a man to give to a woman or girl from whom he expects unqualified obedience and support, but it boded poorly for my mother and myself. So did its corollary: If you can never put yourself first, you can never express yourself. Art becomes, by definition, impossible.

By now I have, of course, broken both commandments many times over. Today, when publicity is the sole requirement for celebrity, celebrity is the ambition of children who once would have opted for something more specific like fireman or prizefighter, and publicity or the fantasy of it is both grease and balm for practically everyone's life, my father's code sounds ludicrous. To follow it would require monumental, self-destructive self-denial, together with the delusion of belonging to a vanished crowd, a family or class that doesn't need any recognition from the outside world.

That was in fact my father's idea of our family and our class, which was pure haute-bourgeois but in his mind was far above that. He saw us as a self-contained aristocracy of intellect, taste, and stoicism, and imbued us with this image. It's an attractive one, if you're inside it, but it's also self-destructive. It encourages a simplistic response to social or emotional complexity: withdrawal into a fortress of self-regard. Together, the image and the code prohibit not only self-promotion but any kind of demand for recognition, even those that are legitimate and essential for survival. In the end they produce a sort of Appalachia of the psyche; emotional isolation disguised as aristocratic hauteur.

I'm amazed that my grandmother Sara didn't break the antipublicity commandment herself, considering her local notoriety and the penchant of small-town newspapers for gossip. The neighbors must have considered her something fairly special; at a time when most women spent all day at home just keeping up with the chores, she would stoke up her fireless cooker, a kind of preelectric crockpot with a heated stone in the bottom, and drive off to antiques sales around the countryside, returning home in time to put the cooked dinner on the table. She ran the family finances, her home, her two sons, and her business.

Did she run her husband? She certainly disparaged him.

When they got older she used to call him "old woman," because he was once mistaken for one by some people whose car broke down in front of my grandparents' house late one night. They knocked on the door and my grandfather, not a tall man and by then rather frail, answered the knock in his nightshirt and old-fashioned nightcap.

Women usually disparage a man out of frustration and disappointment. If my grandmother had at first thought my grandfather was the kind of go-getter the brand-new century seemed to be breeding, she was certainly disappointed. She was the go-getter. Since she was free to run her business and household as she wanted, she might have been perfectly happy with their unorthodox marriage, but she was a woman of rigorous conventions and less imagination than a woman who picked out my grandfather ought to have had. Secretly she was probably dissatisfied with herself as well as her husband, because she thought he should be strong in the practical, down-to-earth ways in which she was strong—the ways in which, by convention, men, not women, were supposed to have the edge. She didn't run him, though, even if he did generally retreat rather than confront her.

My grandfather Frank read seven languages, including Sanskrit, and he preferred the company of books to that of the local gentry—or even, perhaps, his wife. He was famous for getting up in the middle of company and, without a word of apology, retreating to his study, which was sacrosanct, even to Sara. He was eccentric in other ways, too; he had come to Gettysburg to teach engineering at the college, but he had more fun with the art history course he started, using color reproductions he had brought back from Europe and mounted himself on pieces of cardboard. He was probably the only grown man in the whole town who collected arrowheads. My grandmother made him keep his collection in a small, unfinished attic room behind the study, together with his prize Indian hammer, its egg-shaped stone head held onto its willow-stick handle with filthy shrink-wrapped rawhide.

It's not clear where my grandfather got his habits; in a smart but somewhat stolid family, he seems to have been an original. The first family patriarch, Johan Jacob, had arrived in Pennsylvania from Germany in 1749 with a family of craftsman sons, all passages paid in advance. That meant they had some means, as did the fact that they bought land in Adams County from the sons of William Penn, who were selling off their father's royal land grant. Two of Johan's sons fought in the Revolution; the younger, my great-great-great-great-great grandfather Johan Martin, a weaver, may have died in it.

The family became farmers, like practically everyone else in those days, working the rich land north and south of the town of Gettysburg for four generations. And then, as my uncle always said, they could afford to tithe a son to the church, so Jacob Abraham, Frank's father and my great-grandfather, became a Lutheran minister, and after a long career moved back to Gettysburg to teach at the Theological Seminary, up on the ridge made famous by the Battle of Gettysburg.

Jacob Abraham was a powerful patriarch. Frank graduated from Midland College in Nebraska while his father was its president, just as my father later took his degree under

Frank. The family story is that Frank moved to Gettysburg and took up teaching again because Jacob Abraham wanted him home.

A man whose father was that powerful, whose power came straight from God, might well have been shy with his own sons; or maybe Frank just kept his distance from my father and uncle as he did from everyone else. It was a time when parents were raising twentieth-century children on late-Victorian principles; even if they didn't intend to be, fathers were usually pretty remote.

Was my grandfather powerful in his sons' eyes? It couldn't have been easy for either one to have the father heading up the college department in which his son majored. A son entering his father's profession offers a challenge; a father who teaches that son, grades his exams, is liable to apply sterner standards than he might to another student. Certainly he would expect more. But then there was my grandmother's worldly acumen and financial independence, and her vivid contempt for her husband. To a son looking for cues about men and women and their relationships, it must have been extremely confusing.

My father and uncle both chose wives with a conventional domestic bent, whom they could dominate; they also acquired their mother's thoroughly Protestant conviction that making money, earning a living, was the essential thing in life. Anything extraneous to that was a self-indulgence, and self-indulgence was morally unacceptable. My grandfather, who himself had opted for practicality in career and marriage, may have seconded the importance of earning a liv-

ing, even if he was not particularly impressed by the importance of money or the evils of self-indulgence.

His sons carried their mother's contempt for his interests
in their own identities. My uncle was a talented photographer who kept a darkroom for years, but he nearly always
disparaged his work, much of which is superb. Although,
like the rest of the family, he felt himself superior to the
common run of people, he became a country doctor and
ministered all his life to patients he both despised and
envied for their practical, unimaginative lives.

My father, the tough guy, had, like his mother, exquisite
taste in many kinds of objects. When he came home from
Persia during World War II, he brought my mother and me
beautiful filigree silver jewelry and Oriental rugs. (I was
only four, so my rug was a tiny Bokhara prayer rug. Hers was
a Queen Sarouk of the finest quality.) He brought us
enameled wooden boxes filled with tiny Persian miniatures,
enamel on ivory, scenes of languorous hunters pulling bows,
long-skirted courtiers arranged in graceful profile. There
were enameled ivory bracelets and delicately detailed silver
demitasse spoons, and even a graceful army souvenir: a
small, delicate, white silk handkerchief embroidered with
the emblem of the Persian Gulf Command, a green shield
with red star and crescent.

But this stuff was in a sense all trade goods, too—
offerings made to natives of uncertain temperament. My
father's attitude toward taste was what he thought a
nineteenth-century British gentleman's would have been:
valuable as an attribute of a cultivated man of the world, but

when you got right down to it counting for very little. Taste was merely useful in furnishing a home, or buying gifts for women, or ordering suits from one's tailor. One did not take seriously the notion of an aesthetic vision that might color all or even some of life. The pleasure it might provide would be both unimportant and, in the long run, suspect.

My father, the son of an intellectual, believed above all in being "tough-minded." His literary taste ran to Kipling; he had no time for painting or poetry or liberal politics or feminism, the things my mother cared about. He trusted numbers, believed they could not lie; thought words beyond the strict report of fact were false. Thought himself incapable of rigging statistics. To deal with complex problems of identity or politics, he clung to his homilies. Despite his nineteenth-century gentleman's poses, he was an early-twentieth-century man, with the early-twentieth-century American attitude toward work, toward earning your own way and pulling yourself up by your bootstraps, Horatio Alger-like, even if you hadn't started poor. His passions were for work and money, the railroad, and his own ambitions. He was determined to be the man his mother would take seriously—hard-driving, financially acute, a practical businessman. A Republican.

Although he entered the same profession as his father, he shaped himself very differently. My grandfather had designed bridges; my father serviced them. My grandfather had specialized in imaginative solutions to difficult jobs all over the world: The materials for one railroad bridge in Peru had to be carried in over mountain trails by men on foot, so he designed a bridge made entirely of fifty-pound components. No one could accuse my father of such work; he kept the tracks, the rolling stock, and the schedules in shape so that the trains could run on time. He chose to be an engineering maintenance man.

But he was courting my mother, so he listened to what she said about art, or appeared to. He sent her the letters and gave her the books. But he was secretly contemptuous of her family's aesthetic and socialist ideals, because they were of no practical use. As he saw it, he was rescuing her from her dreary life as a legal secretary, from her father's failure to support her properly. He could promise her financial stability and worldly position as the wife of a successful man. Of course he couldn't be called successful yet—his job, barely gained before the full Depression hit, was precarious. But he was ambitious, and he believed he would be a success.

(He never got over the fact that his father-in-law had not been able to afford to keep my mother in college. For his own children, he insisted on paying in full for private colleges unless we won academic scholarships. When I asked him whether I should apply for financial aid on my college application form, he said, "No, I make too much money." You could see that he thought that was the kind of thing any reasonably successful man ought to be able to say.)

When he talked to my mother about the railroad, he was genuinely enthusiastic. He loved the institution and all its objects, loved the beautifully designed Pullman cars, the raw power of the great steam engines, the clean, acrid, oily smell and dull blue sheen of steel.

He loved bossing the men, too, and the camaraderie of the crew. His men liked and respected him, he told my mother—and it was true. Later she saw it for herself. He knew how to talk to them, how to command them and keep the right distance from them, yet still join in the jokes and tobacco and sometimes the whiskey and card games. He had a strong, sentimental, nineteenth-century view of the virtues of class, and of the bonds between the classes when they worked together on a common project, like officers and men in a war.

My father would talk to my mother about all these things, and she would think of her father in his studio with his clay and his wooden tools, and in the foundry with the flowing bronze that assumed the shapes of the birds and animals and human heads her father had modeled in clay, and think that both men loved their different objects in the same way.

Neither she nor my father ever spoke of both men's strong urge to control, to shape, to dominate—objects, other men when possible, all women. My mother must have found this dominance attractive, exciting, in both of them; it must have seemed like a form of love. Did Sara ever tell her to make a life for herself, because my father would not give her any help?

My aunt, who knew them both, believed my parents made a marriage of convenience. I think they were drawn by identification, which is easily mistaken for attraction by people who have some confusion about their own identities. Both my parents were at war with themselves: over the value of the imaginative life of the mind versus that of everyday "reality"; over masculinity versus femininity; over inexorable family demands for self-sacrificing duty versus the subversive desire for personal pleasure, personal existence.

The mutuality of their conflicts and confusions made them believe, unconsciously, that they were in fundamental sympathy with each other; consciously, they thought they saw in each other what they wanted. My mother saw a charming but serious man who would support her financially, aesthetically, and philosophically, and would never betray her sexually. He went to church on Sundays, didn't drink to speak of, and was already buying insurance policies. She felt secure; she may have believed that to be love.

My father saw a shy, diffident, unworldly girl, well bred, with good family roots even if her own father had taken the wrong path. He liked her lack of assertiveness, and thought he was charmed by her aesthetic and socialist ideals; his mother was as strong and practical and worldly a woman as he wanted to know. He never had felt quite up to the mark with her. With my mother, he had immediately felt successful, competent, worldly, strong; all that a man should be. He expanded, and he may have mistaken that expansion for love.

Both my parents were practiced at deception, of themselves even more than others. They were complex, devious, and subtle, living secretly inside labyrinths of feeling they could neither admit nor express. Their marriage would be a stage on which to act out their internal conflicts, but they approached it with their illusions, delusions, and denials intact, trusting in the promises of the culture that if they took this step their lives would be fulfilled.

SEVEN

In the Realm of the Senses

MY PARENTS were both highly sexed, and uneasy about it.

My mother valued the calm surface of control. She loved the light, pure, aesthetic pleasure of shaping her material, smoothing and disciplining the rough lump of wet clay to a serene beauty. But if art is a progression from formlessness to form, sex is the opposite. It starts with two fully clothed, rational human beings and proceeds to break down all control, all form, violating the boundaries that make dignity possible and ending in dishevelment and sweaty nakedness.

My father, who also valued control above all, found it necessary to assign blame. My uncle remembered him as a very young man, long before he had even met my mother, walking down the street behind a couple of girls whose hips and buttocks rode their legs like waves on the sea. Aroused, my father was furious; "What do they think they're doing, walking around like bitches in heat? They shouldn't be allowed out."

My father approved of my mother's ability to sublimate; my mother liked the fact that my father was a prude.

They were probably both virgins, although it is not impossible that my father had been initiated somewhere, perhaps by some friendly whore in Tennessee, set up for him by the surveying crew to celebrate his graduation from stake boy to map-drawer. Still, the wedding night was probably as awkward as the first time anywhere, he perhaps impatient, she ashamed of her own powerful feelings.

No doubt a daughter should not speculate on such things, but my father always took a certain license with me. Oh, it wasn't what you think, not like today's sexual abuse, full-scale coitus for years, and then the daughter takes out a contract on her father's life. (*Coitus* was the word you looked up in the Encyclopedia Britannica, 11th edition, but still couldn't understand because the definition was so oblique and convoluted. It was also the word the sex manual used, the one with the little drawing of the pessary, which sounded like a cross between homemade apple jelly and a wild pig.)

If my father had had coitus with me, I wouldn't have needed to look up the word. His style was slyer. He had many appetites, and he liked to convert the little ceremonies of daily life into occasions for their satisfaction. He loved eating, was master of the rituals that surrounded dinner in those days: fixing the drinks, pouring the wine, carving the roast. As he cut, the slice would curl slowly over toward the juice welling up in the tree of drainage channels on the platter. He would spear it deftly with his carving fork and allow it to hover briefly in the air, dripping, so we could see its color, its grain, before sliding it gently onto the plate held out by my mother—or, later, my stepmother—on his left.

After dinner he would pluck a cigar from its humidor, roll it between his fingers, and listen to the crinkly music it made. (He was tone deaf, but his fingers could feel the sound of good tobacco.)

He drank his liqueur from a small, narrow glass whose thick base was veiled in smoky tones. When he held the glass up, the liquid amber light shone through the drifting smoke like fire. He would hold the first sip in his mouth, rolling it slowly over his tongue until it trickled gently down his throat. Mingled fumes of liqueur, black coffee, and tobacco infused his mouth, sent his whole body into a sweet state of well-being. These were a gentleman's pleasures; they gave away nothing of himself to a women.

By the time I was an adolescent he had other pleasures, less gentlemanly. He liked to loll away summer Sunday afternoons in bed, naked under the sheets, the door to the bedroom always open. Next to him my stepmother sat up decorously in her nightgown. Near her side of the bed—the far side—two chairs and a round table were arranged to create the effect of a sitting room, a conversational grouping with her as anchor. She expected any of us children who were home—by that time, I was the only one still living there—to drop by for a chat.

Both of them expected me to cut through their room to the bathroom we all shared; if I went around by the hall they thought me unsociable. But if I went through their room, I had to pass close to my father, and as I went by he would shift his body just enough to push the sheets askew and give me a flash.

A small thing, yes; a mere lewd wink, a little reminder of father-daughter complicity. My father would never have admitted to it; he believed in getting up early and taking a cold shower. He was convinced that puritanical sternness and strict rectitude kept his appetites in check.

He was like his immigrant ancestors sailing from Germany in the cramped wooden eighteenth-century ship, who had paid their own passage and slept in cabins, but still had to endure the cold and damp, the smell of vomit in the passageways and in their own bunks. They did it on will. Their Lutheran faith bore them up, but with will they could judge how much comfort to take in each other, and whom to condemn when something went wrong.

With a sufficiently strong will, you can ignore the stomach still queasy after the ship has docked; ignore the racing pulse, the clammy palms, the brain buzzing at five o'clock in the morning, when sleep is driven away by the judgmental eye turned inward. At such times my father would spend meditative hours on the toilet, reading the paper, as if to balance the necessity of giving something out with the soothing inward flow of salient fact.

He was a sensual man who had inherited a deep confusion between coolness and coyness. He had seen nothing warmer between his parents, received nothing more affectionate from his mother than a peck on the cheek. Sara had undoubtedly visited on him the usual middle-class Victorian strictures against touching himself. Yet to both her boys she was a tease.

My uncle never talked about this with me, but his son, my cousin, has told me how she played my father and uncle off against each other, as later Sara played off my cousins and brothers. She wanted them to compete for her favors. When her sons were little, she might say things to my father like, "Your brother is getting much better grades than *you* did in second grade," and laugh girlishly. When they grew up, she might ask my uncle, "Do you know your brother just got another promotion?" My uncle's patients paid his fees more often in food than in money: a turkey or a haunch of venison, a bushel of potatoes or basket of cherries. Sara would prod him: "You ought to insist that they pay before you perform any services. John gets a regular salary, you know. He can afford to have three sons." More girlish laughter.

My uncle, the younger brother, clung to the notion of a certain distance from all this. My father was the elder, the more seduced by their mother. He went home to her more often, driving the family to Gettysburg on Sundays whenever we lived close enough, bringing the bottle of Bristol Cream sherry and the good cigars, whose dried butts my grandmother laid under her Turkey carpets and in the corners of her velvet-lined corner cabinets against the moths.

Upstairs, in his study, my grandfather kept his secret life. When he died, Sara preserved everything precisely as he had left it, down to the books on the shelves and the set of Chinese checkers her husband used to bring out for his grandchildren. So it wasn't until after she died, many years later, that my father and uncle discovered, hidden behind the rows of respectable engineering and art-history treatises, a considerable library of exotic pornography in most of the languages my grandfather read, including Sanskrit. My uncle claimed to have been amused by this discovery, but my father was outraged, as though he had uncovered evidence that his father had been cheating on his mother all those years and had gotten away with it.

THE CUES my mother learned were equally confusing. Her father included women among his pleasures. Trygve was heartily, unashamedly physical: his face was ruddy from the sun and his eyes crinkled with laughter. His hands and forearms were thick and sensual. He smelled of the sultry perfumes of linseed oil and paint, the sharp, dank, earth-odor of clay. He loved women, and they adored him. Except for his wife, he never took them seriously; he took them for what they were—diversions. He thought a daughter was there to be charmed, so he charmed her, along with the others at those long dinner tables under the summer trees. She waiting shyly for some sign of recognition, pleased if he waggled the bottle at her in a teasing toast.

Trygve didn't like my father much; he thought there was something a little cold, a little calculating about him. Nevertheless, they got along over the dinner table, as men do; John told railroad stories and Trygve told Norwegian stories and artist stories, and they had their wine and liqueur, two men of the world. My mother liked watching them; she felt warm, included. She made a mistake common to women: she believed that the lazy self-pleasuring of the table and, later, of the bed, were forms of generosity.

This is an easy mistake for a woman to make. If you're eating at the same table with the chief eater, you're bound to feel warm and included. If you've got a live man in your bed, who wraps himself around you and makes you feel terrific, it's easy to believe you have a generous person, someone who will notice you afterward. When such a man turns on the charm, a woman hungry for notice can't see that his main concern is his dinner, and that he expects her to feed him. Or does see, and is willing to comply, believing that it will get her something in return.

My mother understood nothing of the ruthlessness of sexuality—her father's, her husband's, or her own. My father came on bluff and hearty like Trygve, charming her, yet was a misogynist and a prude. He wanted service from a woman, and pleasuring, in his narrow way. He could be sly in getting what he wanted, and cruel, even vindictive, when he didn't. Something in my mother that was cold, already congealing, went out to him. Something cold in them both found familiar territory.

MY MOTHER's coldness was bred as much by her charming father as by her mother. Trygve and Emma came from a far northern country, where the rigors of the climate drove people into a loneliness of the body that fostered stoicism and reserve. In a cold climate, the weaknesses of the flesh are harder to forgive: its outpourings, its tenderness, its shameful needs for touch, warmth, sustenance, rest. Control, or the illusion of it, is drummed into infants and children. Especially girl children, men by and large having always had tacit permission to reach out from their loneliness, to pleasure themselves and appease their appetites. Although men have also had to learn reserve; Trygve and Emma were cool with each other in public and in front of the children.

And even though they had chosen to live in a temperate place, they raised their daughter to a cold standard. My mother learned early to distance herself from her flesh. Nevertheless, she was highly susceptible to all the pleasures of the senses, and Trygve and Emma supplied a feast for her eyes and hands—as long, presumably, as those hands touched clay or wood or the carver's tools, and not her own body. It was inevitable that she would come to exalt the aesthetic response as a form of pure feeling, the opposite of physical passion, and that the aesthetic realm would provide a refuge from the limits, the imperfections, the frequent grossness of the flesh.

Educated girls had long learned to sublimate with art; the tender nudes of Renoir and Manet, the tender boys and men of the classical Greeks, the pale goddesses of the French Academy. By my mother's day, a certain austerity had crept in; Picasso splintered the figure the year she was born, and during her girlhood cubism completed the job. (If her parents took her to the Armory show, she saw Duchamp's *Nude Descending a Staircase* when she was seven years old.) By her adolescence American art, on its way to abstraction, had taken up industrial imagery, the hard-edged planes of precisionism. Its blend of the aesthetic and the ascetic obviously appealed to her, since it influenced her work on the woodcut that hangs on my wall.

By the time she was twelve or so, intimations of her own sexuality would have begun to trouble my mother, and her father's womanizing may have become a painful question. With a philosophy of lofty, pure sensuousness, of appetite subordinate to art, she could hang on to her ideal father, transmute his selfishness to selflessness, see his life as a noble sacrifice to his art. Although she had internalized his attitudes—taking her own talents and skills lightly; preferring Olaf, the son, even though she was the gifted artist; assuming that charm was all she needed or deserved—her philosophy allowed her the illusion of compensation for her father's careless disregard, that had so casually deprived her of the right to make demands on him, or on any man, and so had deprived her of that strong sense of herself on and of the earth that might have enabled her to take herself seriously enough to stay alive.

ONE NOVEMBER afternoon in the thirties, before I was born, my mother and father posed for photographs at his parents' house in Gettysburg. She wore a stylish dark dress, perhaps a wool crepe, in black or navy blue, with four white buttons along one shoulder and a thin line of white eyelet embroidery at the neck and along the button placket. He wore a dark suit, the jacket open to show his white shirt (it was a sultry, southern-Pennsylvania November, too warm for a vest), and smoked a cigar.

In one photo, they stand side by side on the front porch. Naturally they are not touching. She is smiling broadly, showing her upper teeth with the one crooked incisor. My father is smiling a little smugly, his closed mouth swelling his cheeks with its stretch. It is the smile of a man, a son, whose job seems at last secure, whose very presentable wife has produced three sons.

But if you cover up their mouths with your hand, you see at once that neither of them is really smiling. My father's eyelids are narrowed, and in his eyes there seems to be a cool and rather nasty challenge, a thirties' movie-gangster challenge: "Don't fuck with me baby, because I'm calculating your weak points."

The smile in my mother's eyes turns into a trick of the light: a highlight on the outside edge of her right iris, a transparency on the inside edge of her left one. You notice the frown creases running up from the inside edges of her eyebrows, and the dark shadows smearing the inner edges of her eyes. And you see that, just as in all the other pictures of her you possess, her eyes are veiled, as if a scrim has come down behind the pupils, and the person inside is looking at something private projected onto it. Whatever she has learned from my father in marriage, it has not made her less guarded.

There are shots of each of them alone. My father stands on the front porch, grinning toothily but narrowly, with sexy, smiling eyes. He is looking up triumphantly, like a winning politician on election night.

My mother sits indoors, in a wing chair, looking down and slightly away from the camera. She has high cheekbones and a gracefully shaped mouth. She would almost be beautiful, if her Norwegian nose didn't thicken and turn up a little too much at the tip. Her mouth looks resigned, and you can see that the frown lines, or lines of perplexity, are permanent. The overwhelming effect is of sadness, or deep melancholy.

I remember this look; she wore it a lot when I was a child. It was her most private face. When I came upon it, I would feel as if I had blundered into a closed room, seen something that was not meant for me to see. She seemed to be willing herself into some other state, some other time or place, but where it might be I could not guess. I only knew that it was not with me.

EIGHT

The Home Front

THE TIMES when I could be close to my mother on something like comfortable terms usually involved the kitchen, or clay, or the garden, or a book. When we made the terra-cotta animals in the fireplace, or she read a story to me at bedtime, or let me knead bread dough, there was something between us. But when there was nothing to take my attention and focus her into some remembered pattern of caring and of calm, I made her nervous. She needed a lot of space around her; most of the time she kept her distance or turned her back. If I intruded, I might bring down her wrath. It was strict discipline for a toddler; I kept my eye on her, and she kept her back to me.

I WAS not yet two when, in the spring of 1942, my father was commissioned a major in the army and sent out to Fort

Wayne, Indiana, to train a battalion of railroad men for the war. My mother found a little house in a development on the edge of town and moved us all out there.

My father spent most of his time out at the airfield where, for some reason, his army battalion was stationed. Soon he would leave for Persia, where his men would run jeeps, tanks, trucks, guns, food, and ammunition north to supply the Russians, who were about to launch a counterattack against the Germans at Stalingrad, and whose only other outside supply line, the Murmansk ship convoys strung out across the North Atlantic, was a flock of ducks for the German U-boats. My father didn't yet know where he was going, of course, but he was excited about the prospect of going somewhere. He'd been working hard for the railroad, never knowing, through the layoffs of the thirties, whether his name might come up next. The war must have seemed to him like a vacation. He was thirty-eight, he had a wife and four children, and now he was being given the chance not only to return full time to the company of men, to a replay of the great days of school and teams and fraternities, but to help save the world in the process. It was heady stuff; no wonder he seldom came home. My mother was already a war wife, raising three boys, aged six to thirteen, and one girl, me, by herself. She was poised to wait out a war the length of which no one could predict, a thousand miles from her family and anything familiar.

She spent her evenings writing letters. In those days mothers were the family chroniclers; it was something to do at night. My mother recorded everything; my oldest brother's cold, an eclipse of the moon my father had come home to see, my progress in talking. To her in-laws, she apologized for my father, to whom letter-writing was not a priority; "He was sleepy; he wanted to write to you, but couldn't think of anything to say." Normally letters contained photographs of the children, but when the men left, there was no one to take them. My uncle, the doctor/photographer, was a Marine somewhere in the Pacific. "Perhaps you will have the luck I had," my mother wrote my aunt. She had given a lift to a soldier who turned out to be a professional photographer: "he stopped by and took a roll of the children. The ones of Signe are splendid, I think." She enclosed some prints.

A letter is a kind of performance, a little verbal image of yourself you send out into the world. My mother's letters sound like those of any normal, loving, harried wife and mother. To my aunt, she wrote, "I know you are making a heroic effort to keep your mind occupied, but it must be tough. I see the days ticking by so quickly—and then I'll be doing the same." The battalion had had its dance and its open house; my father scrawled a postcript that he was about to leave for Washington, "enroute overseas, I don't know where." And then he left, and for a good part of the next three years my mother was completely alone with us children, in the flatland of northeastern Indiana.

War wives could do nothing at all about being stranded with the kids, with no man in sight if they were determined to be faithful (and not many if they weren't), but they weren't allowed to feel abandoned, or resentful; the war had to be won, and they had to do their part. Officers' wives couldn't go off to California with the kids and sign on as

Rosie the Riveter, either. The right response was the macho one: stiff upper lip, grace under pressure, make the heroic effort. My mother, of course, was used to that.

Very small children sense what's really going on with their parents: I could feel my mother's anxiety, and I could feel her retreat after my father left for Persia. She would make a show of liveliness with other adults, and she roused herself for the boys because they were boys. But with me she didn't seem to need to keep up a front.

Or maybe I just noticed more. I remember a weekend afternoon when we children were rehearsing a backyard circus in the driveway of the house next door. We weren't far from where my mother was sitting in a canvas lawn chair in our back yard, but she was looking the other way. When I went over to ask her to pin up the back of the Halloween leopard costume I was wearing (prewar, a hand-me-down from one of my brothers), she turned only part way toward me, keeping her remove. I wanted to tell her that I was to be the lion and have a solo (in the event, the neighbors' red chow dog got the role), but I said nothing, just turned so she could pin up my costume. She did it efficiently, as she did everything, but her mind wasn't anywhere near me or the circus. I could almost taste the acid about her. It was different from the acrid odor of nicotine that permeated her clothes and flesh. It was a sharp, hard, dead-end kind of taste, metallic and brittle. Years later I learned what it was when I tasted it in myself; it was despair, and deep depression.

While my father was overseas, and even before he first left, I was alone with my mother a lot. Erik started school in the fall of '42, so while on weekends the house was full of brothers, the weekdays stretched long and empty, with no one at all between my mother and me. There weren't a lot of activities for us to share, either. My mother, the gardener, made no Victory Garden in the barren little back yard. She planted no flowers in the skimpy beds around the foundation; the most she did was to tend a few small box bushes. She had to take me with her shopping at the Baer Field PX, but I was too small to help with even the most menial cooking tasks. I could watch her singe the pinfeathers from a fresh chicken, but that was about it.

Sunday nights, after a midday dinner, were a time of exquisite tension. We children had cereal for supper and then listened to the serials on the radio: Tom Mix, the Lone Ranger, Straight Arrow. The boys played with toys they had gotten in exchange for cereal-box coupons, or with cardboard cutouts—airplanes, parachutes—they had assembled from the backs of the boxes themselves. My mother would be somewhere in the background. Sometimes, as a special treat, she would make me milk toast— hot milk, crisp hot toast cut into squares, honey poured over all—and sit with me while I ate it. At other times, when she was more preoccupied, I ate my Cheerios with my brothers.

Then it was Monday, and the boys were gone, and I entered my time of uncertainty. All week I would watch her, covertly, while she went about her housework. With a child's urgent sense of fairness, I convinced myself that she was, equally, watching me. That *inside,* she saw me, even when she was turned away. The burning question was, would she turn toward me—and if she did, would she be welcoming, coolly distant, or enraged?

Her rage was terrifying. She could flash out of her distant place with no warning I could understand, as swift and sudden as the Indiana lightning. Everything about her would stand on end, crackling with electricity. She could swarm toward me like the Medusa herself, with hissing snakes for hair, and hands that could kill.

I would concentrate on how to make her aware of me in some way that wouldn't make her angry. When she was preoccupied, I desperately feared making a sound, or a clumsy move, that might provoke her; at the same time, I feared I might miss the moment when she could notice me. Naturally I would have liked simply to ask her for some attention, but things could not be that simple.

I began to make memories. If I was precocious in this, it was because anxiety created an intense need to perceive the patterns in my immediate surroundings so that I could blend in with them—or, at least, not disturb them. Scenes from those years present themselves whole, as if seen through a time-telescope, the small figures moving in the still air on the other side of the lens.

SCENE: My mother is in the far left-hand corner of the living room, sitting at her writing desk, writing letters. She is turned away from me; I can just see the line of her cheek. I am a room's length away, right outside the living-room doorway in the little front hall, playing with a set of gaily painted wooden clowns jigsawed to lock together at the hands and feet. I am building a pyramid with them, each

clown holding other clowns or hanging precariously, canti-
levered dizzily out into space. The game is virtually silent, as
long as the pyramid doesn't collapse. By not playing on the
living-room carpet I am tempting fate, but I play skillfully. I
fit the clowns together and stand them up, and they don't
fall. I look at the angle of my mother's cheek, and back at the
clowns, and dismantle the pyramid very carefully.

SCENE: the dining room, to the right of the front hall. In
the back left-hand corner is the kitchen door. It's open; my
mother is standing at the sink, washing vegetables. Her back
is to me. I am drawn to her but afraid to come too close; I
watch her from the dining room.

I have been playing with one of her bobby pins; I stick it
briefly into the electrical outlet on the wall just to my left.
The feeling is amazing, a sharp jolt and an unpleasant
tingling. I let go of the bobby pin. All the time I am looking
at her back. She never turns around.

SCENE: I am alone in the living room, in bright sunshine.
My mother is upstairs, taking a nap. The cleaning lady has
been there, and the room is so clean and empty I can't think
of anything to do. The big, shiny, walnut-grained console
that contains both record player and radio is out of the
question, and so is the fireplace with its fantastically noisy
metal tools in their rack.

I'm not supposed to leave the house, but I'm not supposed to touch anything, either. I begin to feel a little
unreal. I decide to brave the back yard. There is a flagstone
walk from the back porch around to the driveway, with little

channels of dirt between the stones. A plastic battleship belonging to one of my brothers lies on the grass; I pick it up and ease it into a channel, sailing it between two South Pacific islands toward a safe harbor, away from the Japanese mines in the open water. I am on my knees, the hem of my dress is under my knees in the dry, dusty grass, my left palm supports my weight. I haven't yet learned the art of concealment.

By the time my mother wakes up and comes downstairs I am back inside, but I still have dirt on my knees and dress. I have wiped my palm across my forehead, leaving a broad, dark smear. This dirt drives my mother into a rage.

SCENE: The front hall, in deep shadow on a bright, sunny day because the blinds are drawn against the heat. A neighbor's child rings the doorbell. My mother answers, looming in dark silhouette in the doorway. I stand behind her in the shadowy hallway looking past her bulk to the brilliant sunlight, the grass, the front walk with the scrawny sapling beside it, the other child standing in freedom on the step. I yearn to be outside, but when the other child asks if I can come out and play, my mother tells her no. I can't believe it; there seems to be no reason not to go out. Inside there will be some dark, tedious punishment, some ritual my mother has concocted because I have once again lapsed from the discipline of the body that was drummed into me before this unsettling move. The outside is so close; I can't believe I can't just walk out into it.

But I can only wriggle and try to speak. Inevitably my

voice rises into the shrill whine of the powerless, edged with panic. I repeat, "I want to go out, I want to go out."

My mother closes the door, swings on me, and suddenly we are in a fight, as if we are equals. Then she remembers that she is three times my size and grabs me. I try to pull away, but of course she prevails. We have struggled in silence but she is talking now: her patience is gone, she cannot put up with this disobedience, she is all alone and I have to obey her, have to, she cannot stand it, I will be the death of her.

Somehow, pulling, dragging, resisting, we arrive at the top of the stairs, at the bathroom. My mother is holding on to me with one hand and trying to pull my shirt over my head with the other. It is an impossible task, so she whacks me on the head, and I stop struggling and pull my head down into my shirt, turtlelike, and she deftly pulls the shirt up and off. I've done resisting; she pulls off my shorts and bathes me, scrubbing and talking furiously. I'm very still, wary. She hauls me to my feet and dries me off, roughly, hoists me up with an arm around my waist and carries me to the bedroom.

She deposits me in her bed and moves around the room, pulling the shades all the way down. It is like being trapped with a tiger; she paces the cage, intent on something, some image; she is barely aware of me. I'm afraid that she might pick me up and shake me, altogether forgetting that I'm her daughter.

Finally she goes out, closes the door behind her. I lie quietly, awake, unable to give up my vigil. I can hear my mother downstairs, moving around angrily, banging things, talking to herself. There is no one else in the house. I watch the light change on the shades, from full bright to slanting shadow, and listen as the house quiets, becomes silent. I hear my brothers come home, hear my mother speak calmly to them. The daily skirmishes between my mother and me are unknown to them; they live, I imagine, with a different mother; one who does not hit, who pays attention to them, who notices.

At dusk, after the boys have eaten and are quiet, doing homework or playing outside, the door opens and my mother appears with a tray. She pauses in the doorway, looks at me to see whether I am awake. She comes in with the tray, turns on the light, and arranges me sitting up, with the tray across my knees. She strokes my hair, my head sore under her touch, but she doesn't acknowledge what has happened. She says she hopes I won't act like this again, that I should understand that she has to put me to bed when I do.

The effect is that I have been very bad, and my mother has vanquished me to chasten me, calm me, teach me a lesson. But I know that, despite my own whining, it was my mother who went out of control. And tomorrow my brothers will again be away at school and I will again be alone with her. But perhaps tomorrow I will be perfectly good.

MY MOTHER needed to control something, and I was there, under her feet. My body was full of errant impulses; our family was split by war; she was consigned to a stark little

house in a culture-free subdivision with three growing boys who, being boys, were off limits. Oh, she could
take charge of their mouths, occasionally; I still remember
my triumph and terror at seeing her force my archrival
Erik to wash his own mouth out with soap for saying
"damn." But mostly now the boys were testing their muscle. When Hal refused to wear knickers anymore, Arno,
already in long pants, sided with him. She was helpless
against them.

I was helpless against her. She took her stand on my body;
found in its treacherous depths a betrayal of her own deep-
est longings for perfection. She wanted me calm, neat, and
clean. She wanted nothing to come out of any orifice that
was not sanctioned, in timing and in form. Above all, she
wanted nothing to show.

I had learned her lessons before we came to Indiana, but
in the confusion of moving and adjusting to a new place
their hold was too tenuous; my body betrayed me. My
mother declared an all-out war, using every offensive
weapon at her disposal.

Her attack on my ambulatory impulses was straightforward: forbid them, and punish all evidence, whether whining desire or dirty knees. Her assault on my internal
impulses involved laxatives, enemas, forced-marches on the
toilet. She would teach me regulation, perfect control, by
forcing me to lose control. It was a dizzying paradox; too
dizzying for me to take in. I was in love with my body,
feeling it grow, using my legs to carry me away from her. But
I was learning that the black depths of it could never be
trusted and never be forgiven.

MY MOTHER makes many caring gestures: fits me for a little smock dress she is sewing, buys me a teddy bear at the PX. One afternoon she writes down a story I make up about a cow in a field caught in a thunderstorm. She has created a little book by folding a large piece of paper, stitching a spine with ribbon and cutting the pages. On one page she draws my cow for me. I have a debate with myself over whether to end the story sadly, with the cow struck by lightning, or happily, with the sun shining. I know my mother would prefer the sun shining, and I'm a little afraid of the lightning strike, so I opt for the happy ending. My mother sketches in a rainbow over the cow.

In the photographs I am cute: blond, plump, with a ribbon in my topknot. I peek out, smiling, from behind a gate, or am posed against the neighbors' chimney base, just to the right of our driveway.

But when my mother is out of control I feel as if I have been cut in two; half of me is there in a bubble of anger with her, her rage is upon me and in me, becomes one with the bad, wicked stuff of my body, with all my feelings and impulses—with my urge, simply, to be. I believe that I am the reason she goes out of control; it is because of the bad self I carry inside me.

I will make sure that this bad half of me is entirely hidden, out of sight of the good, smiling, pretty little girl in those photographs, who is outside the house, who is the child of her mother's perfection. Even as my mother and I contend, part of me splits off, moves outside the room to the calm of the summer day. She is standing out there, looking in at me. She is my rock.

FINAL SCENE: I learn. One afternoon while my mother is taking a nap, I go out the front door and walk up the street. The little subdivision is quiet in the hot sun. There is no traffic. I walk down a block that contains vacant lots, half dug up, where construction on new homes came to a halt years before, during the Depression. A crater, overgrown with grass and weeds, attracts me and I walk carefully over to its edge. I have heard my brothers talking about their cat, Bootsie, who has run away. I imagine Bootsie, a brown tabby tomcat, to be in the crater, invisible among the weeds. If I found him, I could become a hero, but I am afraid to walk down into the crater, because if I fall there will be evidence on my hands and dress. So I imagine Bootsie suddenly streaking out of the crater toward freedom.

I walk on. Another block of vacant lots, a little scary, and I come to the edge of an older neighborhood, with big houses set well back from the street and large shade trees in the yards. The houses are painted different colors; the one nearest me, on the corner across the street, is dark green, with a big front porch. I hesitate on my side of the street; if I am seen here it will constitute evidence of a sort. But I am drawn to the houses and trees; they are very different from the mean, shadeless little boxes of the subdivision. I imagine myself strolling up the walk toward the green house. When I get to the shade of the clump of pines in the front yard, I feel the deep mystery of tree-space, more satisfying than church, the cool dry odor of pine bark, a room enfolded by soft-looking green needles. I could sit there in the shade, or the front door of the house could open and a mother would be standing there, with a pitcher of lemonade

99

and a smile and a hug, like the radio mothers or the ones in the magazine pictures. Inside the house there would be a different life.

After a while I turn and retrace my steps along the baking sidewalks. I hear a drone in the distance, a plane noise but different, more leisurely than the urgent, high-pitched sound of the fighter planes that sometime buzz our house, showing sharks' teeth or pinup girls painted on their noses. A small, plump blue plane appears, skinny wheel struts splaying out under its fat body. As I look up, a door suddenly opens in the plane and the sky is filled with a dark cloud of something that obscures the sun for a second and then disintegrates into separate sheets cascading to the ground.

They fall around me. I pick one up and look at it. It is orange, with black marks on it. I know they are letters. I can make out a few words, an "and" and an "of." The paper has a nice weight and grain, rather coarse; I stick a corner in my mouth, moisten it with spit. It tears away easily and I chew on it as the flyers drift and blow around me.

NINE

Travels in
Arabia Deserta

I'LL TELL you something: By the time my mother killed herself, I liked her better than I ever had. The battles of the body were a long way behind us; I had repressed them. I had reached high childhood, when a girl is both competent and mobile, and has not yet been betrayed by her flesh into sexuality and death. I was immaculate, and free. And my mother had been trying to do something for me; to educate me after her own fashion. She had sent me to a teacher for French lessons and bought a piano.

The French teacher was a real Frenchwoman, an exchange teacher at the high school who lived, exotically, in an apartment in Wayne, our town, one stop down the line from St. Davids, where by this time we had been living in our big Victorian house for two or three years. Everyone around there lived in houses; the only people I had known in apartments were families who couldn't afford houses or elderly widows who no longer needed them. I didn't know any other women living alone who weren't old.

The Frenchwoman was young. She would greet me at her door on Saturday mornings in a peignoir, my first encounter with that glamorous word. Once I was installed at her kitchen table, laboriously copying phrases into my notebook, she would head for the telephone in the living room. She spoke French, but I eavesdropped anyway; I loved the sound of it. The curtained glass door was shut part way, but I could see the tip of one pink satin mule and occasionally a hand, a wrist, and part of a satin sleeve when she reached for another cigarette. She was my first crush. Everyone said she was involved with the handsome exchange teacher from Sweden, and I imagined them saying incredibly romantic things to each other, she in French, he in Swedish, each, miraculously, understanding the other.

At about the same time, an old walnut upright piano appeared in our living room, with *John Thomas's First Book for Children* on the music rack. Fay, the teenage daughter of the Irish justice of the peace in the twin house next door, taught me scales, and I happily banged out "Chopsticks" and "Volga Boatman." For a brief, heady period I felt special; a proper girl, the equal of any boy. My mother's daughter.

My mother was in her up period—believing, with the rest of us, that my father had finally had his last transfer, and that his next move would be vertical, to a vice president's office in the Pennsy's headquarters building right there in Philadelphia. She had decorated her house and made her gardens; now she was cooking and baking up a storm and still had energy for politics. She joined the League of Women Voters, and in the '48 election sat as an official at a trestle table in front of the voting machine installed in the Victorian toolshed (complete with Gothic gables) under a big hemlock tree in a corner of the justice of the peace's front yard.

We were all acting like a family. On late spring and summer evenings and on weekends, my father would help my mother tend her gardens, changing into khaki workclothes and the heavy, lace-up ankle boots he called clodhoppers. He was cheerful and sweating, putting up poles for the beans to climb on. For some reason, manual labor brought out the best in him. Like my mother, he was patient when working with objects, willingly giving them the careful attention they required. He would demonstrate his techniques to any of his children who happened along, and drink quarts of my mother's iced tea.

He had made some big financial investments in the house: he had the upper floors insulated, an exciting process involving three men, a big pump, lengths of wide, flexible tubing, and acres of loose fiberglass. And he had a huge pit dug in the side yard, the mounds of dirt next to it serving as a neighborhood playground until a 3000-gallon oil tank was installed so that we could get rid of the coal furnace. The oil company said it was the biggest tank they had ever filled. The scale was typical of my father, who didn't stint on his own comforts. He must have figured he'd get a bargain buying oil in bulk, while his huge reserves would shield him from price fluctuations.

My brothers flourished. Arno played football for the high school, sang in the chorus, and acquired a steady girlfriend, the one he eventually married, to whose mother my mother later mentioned her despair. Hal joined a boy scout troop that met in a real log cabin in the woods, graduated from a BB gun to a real rifle, and went hunting. Erik inherited the BB gun and perforce joined the cub scout troop that my mother, an inveterate den mother where her youngest and favorite son was concerned, started for him. (He never used the BB gun, while I, who was not allowed to touch it, naturally coveted it.)

I came into my own as a child, at last. When we moved in, and I was installed in the remote little back second-floor bedroom, my father stuck glow-in-the-dark stars on the ceiling so I wouldn't feel so lonely. He and my brothers pitched in to build a sandbox frame against the old carriage-house wall in the back yard and hang a homemade board swing on thick rope from the big old maple tree next to it. Sand was trucked in to fill the sandbox, but it and my bedroom were too isolated and too vulnerable to ambush; I had my eyes on other turf.

I finally went to first grade, real school, my dream for as many years as I had been conscious. And I was free to roam the vast world of our neighborhood, bounded on each end by local railroad stations: ours, St. Davids, about a quarter-mile's walk toward Wayne; the other, Radnor, a half or three-quarters of a mile in the other direction. As a railroad family, we had passes and rode the train, the Paoli Local, about a mile to school in Wayne. All the conductors, burly men in stiff hats of dark blue cloth with the red-and-gold

Pennsylvania Railroad keystone emblem mounted above shiny bills, knew my father and greeted me by name.

When I went to school I thought I would become as important in life as my brothers; would be both noticed and respected. My buoyant mood made me a success. I made a best friend and began to learn my way around in the peer-politics of first grade, negotiating over the block corner or the post office. I learned how to impress the teacher without losing face with the other kids, and, when the time came to read, led a small group in revolt against *Dick and Jane*.

We were mostly youngest children, ambitious and competitive, who had already taught ourselves to read, or had been taught, casually, by older people in our families. I had learned the alphabet in my family's letters-on-road-signs game, but I had learned to read words because my little bedroom, next to the bathroom, at the foot of the stairs to the boys' dormitory, was a natural meeting place; brothers, or even my father or mother, waiting to get into the bathroom, would stop in to hang out, fool around, maybe read nursery rhymes aloud. I learned the rhymes by heart and would recite them along with the reader. I taught myself to read by poring over the pages and matching what I knew was there with the words I saw, then trying out my skill on the next reader who came along.

At school my work didn't go unrecognized; eventually, to keep us quiet, my first-grade teacher gave us real books, with stories. But we still had to take our turns at reading aloud that despised minimalist prose in which Dick and Jane and the rest of the family performed their pathetically limited activities.

I was insatiably hungry for people. I began to make friends of my own in the neighborhood, some of whom my mother didn't know. I learned to exploit one of the great opportunities open to children: hanging around. A canny child can fit right in with almost any family; there is always playing to be done or an animal to be looked after or a snack or even a meal to be eaten. There are adults to be exploited: generous or merely tolerant mothers, retired couples whose own children are grown, childless couples. Adults liked me; I gave good value. I was quick, had a lively imagination and a sense of humor, and knew how to be charming. I was, altogether, a successful child.

I was also privileged. We had a cleaning lady and a woman to do the ironing, so very little was expected of me in the way of chores. Outside of school, meals, and bedtime, I was almost completely free. My mother still took a nap every afternoon, but I no longer worried so much about whether she discovered that I had taken off. Sometimes she seemed not to notice, or care. Once or twice a week she would become upset and confine me to our yard, but I had only to wait until she had gone upstairs for her nap to sneak out to freedom.

The neighborhood was wildly eclectic, bordered by big estates, with pockets of blue-collar families in small row houses and an apartment building down toward Radnor Station, and the large houses of the haute bourgeoisie at our end. I made my rounds impartially, happily running up and down both the cast-iron outside stairway of the apartment building in which whole families shared a few rooms, and the carpeted indoor staircases of the big neo-Georgian or

Tudor houses that had maids and many bedrooms. I visited the man rumored to have married his housekeeper after his wife died, and I took ice cream on summer evenings with the retired couple who liked to show me their home movies. The daughter of a Baptist minister became one of my best friends, the daughter of Sicilian immigrants another.

Theresa Lentini, whose parents spoke no English, was a few years older than I but, I thought, much more naïve. She had three older brothers, though, so we understood each other. She lived only three doors from me, in a small brick house at one end of our Victorian enclave. We spent a lot of time engineering escapes from her chores and her ever-vigilant mother, whose world consisted of cleaning, washing, and cooking for her men (in ascending order of time consumption) and who regarded Theresa as her apprentice. When I was grounded we had two mothers to evade, and we would creep along hedges and cut across back lots until we were out of sight of both houses and could emerge to stroll boldly down the street to the candy store in the little gas station near Radnor Station.

The store was a dark cave several steps below street level. Its rough, white-painted stone walls were covered with tattered ice-cream and soda posters, and the old wooden counter was jammed with big jars of licorice and jelly beans, the March of Dimes canister, stacks of local pennysavers, and rotating wire racks holding vertical rows of clips or hooks from which were suspended key chains, little bags of jerky or potato chips, packets of aspirin and Alka-Seltzer. On a hot summer day we would cut across the boiling tar of the tiny gas station lot, once the owners' front yard, with its single pump standing between their front door and picture window. We would walk down the steep steps to what had once been their cellar, push open the scarred wooden door, plunge into the shade and coolness, say hello to whoever was behind the counter, the husband or wife or oldest daughter, and keep going to the big freezer against the opposite wall. Raise the lid and plunge our hands in to grope for a Dixie Cup or a Popsicle, letting our fingers play a little, touching a few containers, leaning over to get our faces as close as possible to the cold so we could breathe it in.

Whenever I could, though, I hung around Mrs. Lentini's kitchen, because most of the time she was cooking and I got to help Theresa make pasta from scratch without a bowl. This process seemed amazing to me: Theresa would construct a circular flour dike on the enameled-metal kitchen table, pour milk and egg into its lagoon, and gradually demolish the dike as she worked the flour into the liquid. We would shape the springy dough into loaves and feed them through the hand-cranked pasta mill to produce wide, flat lasagne noodles; narrow, flat fettucini; or round spaghetti from angel-hair to thick. We draped the finished noodles over the wooden arms of the towel rack to dry.

When I dared, I would linger on until my mother called up and demanded my presence at home; when I was lucky, Theresa's father, who was the neighborhood gardener, or one or the other of her brothers would arrive and demand to be fed, which usually meant I got a pasta snack. It didn't surprise me that males were fed on demand while Theresa was required to eat at specific times; nor was I ashamed to take advantage of the fact that, as a guest, I could to some extent share male privilege. Theresa could usually ride my coattails and get a snack, too.

My best private-school friend, Judy Marshall, lived not far from the Lentinis, in a neo-Tudor house with a huge third-floor playroom that had window seats and wood-paneled walls with secret doors into mysterious attic recesses. The living room had wall-to-wall carpeting with Oriental rugs on top and chairs upholstered in yellow silk. I never saw Mrs. Marshall actually cook, but she would make tuna salad sandwiches in her modern Formica kitchen and sit at the table to chat with us while we ate them.

Her good-humored attention to Judy fascinated me; I wanted to be a party to their understanding, a member of their alliance. Theresa Lentini and her mother were far more interesting and romantically intriguing; I loved the smells and sights and tastes of their kitchen, and I secretly envied Theresa her mother's fierce presence. But Mrs. Lentini was a paradox; she was clearly the heart of her family, yet Theresa and I agreed that her life was drudgery, to be avoided at all costs. Mrs. Marshall appeared to transcend the mere details of domestic life. She had an air of satisfaction, even power; the bond between herself and Judy appeared to be so secure it was smug. They seemed to be a higher order of woman; I thought they had a privileged exemption from female rules, as I had at the Lentinis.

I couldn't get enough of visiting other people's houses; they were my foreign countries, mysterious, unknown, possibly containing the secrets of the universe. Like some nineteenth-century romantic traveler, I would immerse myself in the daily lives of the people, share their customs, imagine myself to be one of them. Houses I hadn't visited were a challenge; I would look for a chance to insinuate myself into the families that lived in them. I was prepared to accept anything and anyone I found; like a new land to the inveterate wanderer, each house or apartment was a theater for another self, each room a stage on which I could make my exits and my entrances.

In certain moods I would head toward Radnor Station to visit someone very unlike either the Marshalls or the Lentinis, with their richly ordered cultures. Someone like the boy who lived in the big, run-down farmhouse that sat, a presuburban relic, on its own bald little hill, all that was left of its land. Plump, friendly, distracted, my friend's mother seemed to have given up trying to organize her brood and simply sat at the kitchen table, dispensing orange juice from a grimy plastic pitcher to the troops of children who swarmed in and out, all of us grubby, snot-nosed, and rude.

In my private sagas, I was usually a poor child, perhaps an immigrant, making my own soap from lye and ashes like Mrs. Lentini. I spent a lot of time playing in a filthy little room, or shed, under our side porch. It had a single square, glassless window and a doorframe with no door. It was furnished with a makeshift table balanced unsteadily on overlapping scraps of linoleum that didn't quite cover the uneven dirt floor. In one corner ghostly ailanthus trees sprouted among the remnants of a woodpile. I found this combination of grubbiness, poverty, and out-of-the-wayness irresistible. The room served me as playhouse, railroad cab, and ship's cabin; one of my brothers nailed a peach-basket lid to the edge of the doorframe to make a steering wheel. I could play Billy the Kid in his hideout or an innocent orphan, making my own way in life, living alone in a frontier cabin.

I had good times in that little space, mostly by myself. The room was a kind of concrete analogue to the family code of stoicism and asceticism. At the same time, its general griminess and haphazardness was an answer to my mother's compulsive cleanliness and regularity. I seldom took friends there. It was too close to the kitchen window, directly above, to allow private conversation, but I think the real reason was that when I was with friends I saw the room through their eyes, and this made me feel protective toward it and toward myself. In the privacy of silence and solitude, its bleakness inspired my fantasies.

More often than not, I chose to play a boy; I had very early been impressed by the fact that in my family being a girl offered no advantages at all. As the youngest, I was smallest and weakest anyhow; as a girl I was marginal in the family culture. I never played Cinderella; I disliked her passivity in the first part of the fairy tale, and I didn't dare believe in a fairy godmother and prince. Nothing I had learned about being a girl suggested the possibility of rescue. In fact, Cinderella came too close to home. In the fairy tale she was not only the family drudge but also its supernumerary, whose role was to cheer her stepsisters on, to admire their dancing and their new clothes. In my own family, my career as a girl was similar; I spent years as the family supernumerary, spectator and camp-follower to my brothers, whose activities thereby acquired for me a dimension of reality that my own never possessed.

My father or mother used to take us all to my brothers'
cub scout and boy scout merit badge ceremonies, and to the
local jamborees with their ritual demonstrations of prowess
at activities like sliding along a rope in a harness from one
end of the gym to the other. On Saturday afternoons we all
bundled up to go to my oldest brother's football games. My
mother sometimes took me to one or another brother's
scrimmages, on a damp field during chill, foggy afternoons
in November, with a handful of other mothers and little
brothers.

When I was old enough for Brownies, my mother was
busy with Erik's cub scout troop. When she had first led a
troop for him in Fort Wayne, I had been by necessity a
hanger-on at meetings. To keep me busy, she would let me
learn to make papier-mâché or whatever with the boys, then
send me off into a corner to make some simple object, a ball,
out of clay and cover it with papier-mâché, while the cubs
made whatever it was they were making that week. I always
felt that, however much it might have pleased me—and a
bright orange papier-mâché ball is a lovely sight to a four-
year-old—what I made was not real. My mother, busy with
her real work, would usually ignore it; one of the boys might
notice it and say something kind, but I knew it wasn't the
real thing.

So the French lessons and the piano had an immense
significance for me. I was on the verge of having my existence, my reality in the family, confirmed. In school I gravi-
tated naturally to the stage, where my fantasy became the
reality, and everyone watched me act. I would often collabo-
rate with my best school friend, a veterinarian's daughter,

both of us tomboys happy to imagine ourselves Mounties behind dogsleds, pushing tipped-over wooden chairs across the Arctic tundra of the elementary-school auditorium stage.

I had no trouble moving from solitude to company and back, or between the disparate worlds of my friends. Since the sagas that unfolded in my head when I was alone didn't seem any less real to me than the daily life of the families I dropped in on, I could create all the continuity I needed. Still, something eluded me. In each family, real life unfolded before me in discontinuous chapters that yet had a certain eerie sameness. I saw patterns: pasta made in the Lentini kitchen nearly every day, children not allowed in the living room at the Gerhardts across the street, the elderly couple waiting with their ice cream and projector. What I didn't see, but strained to catch, were the details that created people's sense of their own particular, private realities—the things said and unsaid, done and undone, between and around the patterns of custom and habit that were so familiar they were hardly noticed.

I longed to be those people, to capture the minutest elements of their lives. I memorized the layouts of their houses, the furnishings of their rooms. I knew every detail of the antimacassars on the maroon plush living-room suite at the Lentinis, of the old-fashioned wringer washing machine in their basement, next to the splintered wooden shelves lined with pretzel tins full of succulent little filled pastries and brittle, flat, sweet biscuits made on the stove with a small, diamond-shaped waffle iron, all waiting for the aunts and uncles and cousins who would fill the house on the next feast day or birthday. I had helped make those pastries, and I sometimes helped Theresa serve them to the uncles from cut-glass plates, bringing bottles of beer as they settled back after a holiday meal to digest. I would watch in fascination as they unbuttoned the waistbands of their pants to ease the pressure on their paunches.

At odd moments, alone in the Marshalls' playroom, or in the outfield during a late-afternoon softball game somewhere in the neighborhood, while I was doing nothing in particular, not looking for a hit to come my way but just watching the blue shadows lengthen on the grass and noticing how the light changes, becomes softer, cooler and more mauve, a slight blurring of detail giving things a delicacy denied them in the harsh light of full sun, I would experience a kind of exaltation and an intense sense of the fragility of time.

I was amazed at my ability to receive this moment, this precise second of the universe, even as it disappeared forever. But I also felt irrevocably separate, cut off from the sheer, unselfconscious being-with-people I'd enjoyed all afternoon and that everyone around me appeared to be enjoying still. I cherished this sensibility, this melancholy; it expressed my sense of being an outsider, of not having at the center of my own life something that felt like intimacy.

MY MOTHER didn't approve of my eclectic taste in friends; it drove her crazy that I spent so much time with Theresa Lentini. The Main Line was extremely snobbish. The middle classes took their pretensions from their proximity to the great estates, which were already being abandoned when I was a child but whose reputation lingered on, giving the whole area an image of monolithic hauteness, like Westchester or Shaker Heights or Grosse Pointe. My own family, in no way social, was more snobbish than most, with our inbred idea of superiority to everyone—to the common run of upper-class types, with their wimpish dependence on money and pleasure, and the common run of middle-class folk, of whom the same might be said. We went to public school, but we were bound for the Ivy League and the Seven Sisters, while most of our friends would end up at Penn State or Garland Junior College or even Slippery Rock State Teachers' College. "Don't forget, we belong to the upper one-half of one percent in intelligence," Hal told me once when, as an adolescent, I insisted on going out with a boy of whom he disapproved.

My mother was happy enough to plan children's birthday parties with my school friends' conventional, conservative mothers, but on her political committees she consorted with local aristocrats of a decidedly more liberal stripe, many of them Quakers. On the subject of friends of mine like Theresa, she was torn. The middle class had its prejudices; the mother of a high-school cheerleader, a girl in my oldest brother's class, forbade her daughter to go out with one of Theresa's older brothers on the ground that he was Italian. This offended my mother's socialist principles, but in fact she also preferred me to play with other kinds of friends. So she would tell me I was making myself a nuisance at the Lentinis, and ground me, and I would sneak away and follow my own nose.

I was stubborn; we all were. In fact, we were a family of extremists. We each wanted total control: my father over the entire household; each of my brothers in his own world; my mother over me and what she considered to be her own household turf; me over my own time and space. None of us had any idea of the fine points of compromise, of accommodation. Our way of keeping control was to maintain our distance. "See your best friends seldom, and your acquaintances hardly ever," Hal said to me once, years later.

In the family, we had to see each other every day; we dealt with that by keeping our mouths shut. (That was the second half of a favorite army adage of my father; the first half was about keeping your bowels open.)

Once when I was about seven I asked my mother how you knew you were going to have a baby. (I had recently watched one of our cats give birth in the playroom.) "Oh, you just know," my mother said. I was certain it was something that just sneaked up on you, an ambush, like Erik hiding behind the hedge or the couch or under my bed, to tackle me or lob a pillow, or growl and kick up alarmingly after I had reluctantly turned out my light at night. I knew that babies had to do with bodily functions, probably related to something you ate, and in my world all that stuff had always involved ambush and attack.

At the time my mother, of course, was preoccupied with her own projects. Sometimes, as in cooking and gardening, I could enter in. At bedtime she sometimes still liked to read to me. Once in a while I could lure her into playing with me, but her mood had to be just right. Basically my relationship with her still consisted largely of reading her mood and keeping away from her when necessary. But I was becoming more independent; I had more resources of my own. Although she still expected me to be ready to take advantage of moments when she was feeling sociable, I would often rather do things on my own or with friends. I usually preferred reading to myself, a heresy that didn't please my mother when she was in the mood to read to me.

One night when my best school friend was spending the night, we got involved in a water fight in the bathtub. My mother, for whom image counted a great deal, had planned to read to us, and she told us that we had to choose between our water fight and a story. We chose our water fight—or, rather, *I* chose our water fight; since it was my house and my mother, my friend deferred to me. I felt the weight and excitement of my choice; this was my first conscious awareness of the possibility of power in a direct confrontation with my mother, as opposed to circumventing her directives when she wasn't around. I was keenly aware that my position depended entirely on the presence of an ally, but that didn't diminish my feeling of satisfaction in forcing my mother to defer to my wishes.

I could tell that she felt hurt and angry in equal parts, although she reacted only with brisk coolness; she seldom lost her temper with me now that I was bigger, and never in front of someone else. Still, her hurt dashed my pleasure; I felt guilty about depriving her of her occasion. But I also felt she had failed me by forcing me to choose between what I wanted and what she wanted, and then making me feel guilty for choosing what I wanted, as if I could only do so at her expense.

I had already begun to discover that I wasn't really going to get the recognition I had hoped I would earn by going to school. An incident with my first reader, the despised *Dick and Jane,* had been the tip-off. Even though I already knew how to read, the handing out of our first books at school had seemed to me to be a triumph, a recognition, and I had carried my copy home, fantasizing all the way about my mother's proud, happy congratulations. But when I arrived, my book in my outstretched hand, she was on her way out the door with some friends. I tried to show her my prize, but she laughed and said she would look at it later. As she and her friends walked past me across the porch to the waiting car they were all laughing, and my mother was observing, somewhat apologetically, that children always want something at the most inconvenient times.

This, I think, was what I was looking and listening for in other people's lives: some sense that there were worlds in which if you had something it would not immediately be taken away from you. In which more than one person could share the same turf, or people would recognize each others' turf, so that standing your ground didn't always mean isolation and bad feeling.

TEN

After the Peace, the Cold War

MY EARLIEST memory of a gun is of pointing a solid rubber toy .45 at my father. He grabbed it and took it away from me. "Don't ever point a gun at anyone," he said sternly, "not even a toy." I was four or five years old at the time and his advice made no sense to me since I could plainly see that the toy .45 didn't even have a hole in the barrel.

Now I think a sweeping prohibition made sense: you never knew what any of us might do. Since we trusted objects more than ourselves, sooner or later we projected or externalized everything we thought we were hiding onto an object or another person. To me, the objects that most represented us were guns, because our style of violence was mainly to remove ourselves as far as possible, then blast away.

My father understood the lore of guns. He didn't really own guns and I seldom saw him with one, but knowing how to use them, how to control their violence, was for him another of the accoutrements of manhood — certainly of military manhood. And military manhood was his ideal; all those proud pictures of him in uniform. Guns went with those uniforms. Guns beat Hitler and Hirohito and the Indians. John Wayne used guns, and Gary Cooper. Guns were the paradoxical symbols both of power and authority and of freedom and independence. They were about control.

Of all my brothers, Hal, the middle one, the boy scout, was the one who got involved with guns. For as long I can remember, he has collected them in a small way. He always had an antique or two plus some small-bore rifles, a shotgun, and a couple of pistols. I don't think he ever did much hunting; he occasionally went skeet shooting. Mostly he just liked to have the guns and take care of them. Sometimes he would load a couple of rifles in their leather cases, lay them in the back seat of the car, and drive around. He was the middle child among the boys, and like many middle children was generally politic. I think the guns gave him a feeling that there might be a point when he wouldn't have to be politic any more.

Memories of guns: My mother is alive, and we are at the Pennsylvania farm where we spent some summer vacations. My brothers hang a target on a small sapling near the house and blaze away at it with Hal's .22 until the target falls to pieces. I envy their pleasure, but I don't understand it. They have been laughing about the men picking tomatoes in the field next door. Somehow these men are a great joke to them. "Joe White and his Puerto Ricans," they chant, blasting away. They shoot down half a dozen targets before they grow bored and stop. When I go up to the tree, I see that they have pretty well shot it to pieces, too. It all seems wasteful and loud and incredibly violent. I wonder whether Joe White and his Puerto Ricans have heard my brothers talking about them as they shoot.

I have a photograph of myself in blue jeans, sitting on a harrow with the .22, not loaded, across my knees. As with anything connected to my brothers, I covet that rifle, but what I really want is not so much it as the status, the existence, I believe it will confer on me.

This chronic envy makes it very easy for my brothers to play tricks on me. Later that same summer they lure me to explore an abandoned house that stands in the middle of treeless, barren fields. They get me up to the third floor and then run away, leaving me alone in dead space. I can hear their whoops and catcalls, and through the empty windows I watch their moving bodies recede across the bare ground, the only animals visible in the midday sun. I know they think I am frightened, alone in the house, so I'm determined not to be. Anyway, the house seems peaceful and unhaunted—a dry husk, like a gourd. I'm more afraid of an ambush, so I wait for some time in the silence after my brothers disappear behind the tree line at the edge of the fields before I run down the stairs and set out for home, feeling as exposed as the sapling on which they hang their targets.

When I'm sixteen or seventeen, I come home late one

night from a date with my boyfriend; when I open the front door Hal is standing in the dark front hall, pistol cocked. He has gotten up to investigate the sound of a car and people outside. "You're lucky I didn't shoot you," he says cheerfully.

Once, a couple of years after my mother died, our father got us out in the back yard and had us shoot at a target in rounds of three shots each. The idea was to see how close together you could get your three shots; a perfect score would be a single hole dead center in the bull's-eye. A triangle in the bull's-eye was acceptable. Somehow, I did that, in spite of my glasses. Guns make me nervous, but something about the feel of that rifle in my hands, holding it steady against my cheek, aiming down the barrel at the target, had a calming effect. Maybe it was because my father, standing over me, was for once patient. My hands were steady as I squeezed the trigger; I had perfect control.

Cars are the other objects I associate with my family. Thinking of my father makes me think of all those Germans raging down the Autobahn. We, too, judged without mercy, with the absolute conviction of Klansmen condemning a black, or Nazis a Jew; with the unspeakable certainty of righteousness that belongs to the Inquisitor who knows he has God on his side.

Guilt was a condition of our daily life. If something happened, someone had to be blamed. Once when my mother was driving me and two of my brothers home from school the back way, driving slowly because we had just rounded the turn after going under the railroad bridge and a traffic light was coming up, I thought of a ploy to get her attention. There was a big old Victorian house on our left; I was sitting beside her on the front seat. I leaned toward her, looking past her and pointing, and said, "*Look* at that *fantastic* house!" She looked, just for a moment, and then thought she had to stop short to avoid bumping the car ahead, which during her momentary lapse in attention had stopped for the red light but which still had a good twenty-foot lead on us.

For a minute there was a terrible silence. My mother, always a nervous driver anyway, was shaken up. As soon as she had recovered, she spoke sharply to me. Hal took the occasion to announce that I had nearly caused an accident. He and Erik's palpable relief and delight in the fact that this one was clearly my fault was overcast by the knowledge that at some point their turns would come. Like some kind of fate, a black cloud of guilt and depression settled over the car.

Our father's judgment was, of course, even more terrible. On Sundays he would load us all into the Studebaker for a drive. This was supposed to be fun, but he was impatient. While he became enraged at the incompetency of the bitches, bastards, and Sunday drivers on the road, I would cower in the back seat, waiting to be sick. I started feeling dizzy and nauseous soon after I got into the car, especially if it was hot and the car reeked of gasoline, dusty upholstery, hot rubber, and asphalt. I would try to breathe as little as possible.

Inevitably, though, I was sick. The big question was timing. If I announced that I felt sick and asked my father to stop the car, I was instantly in disgrace. If I got out and stood by the road and failed to be sick, I had held the whole family up for no good reason. Perhaps it was a all just a trick; a devious, childish way to gain attention.

If, on the other hand, I waited too long and was sick in the car, I had ruined everything: the car, everyone's Sunday afternoon—and, nearly, my father's control. He would hunch over the wheel while the back of his neck grew redder. My mother, beside him on the front seat, would pass back a handkerchief while we looked for a gas station.

My ideal solution, achieved only once and by accident, was to be sick out the window while the car kept going. My father did not have to be interrupted, there was no mess inside the car, and I was relieved. When we got home, my father hooked up the garden hose and handed it to me.

Needless to say my brothers, on these drives, were all innocence.

ALL THIS emphasis on judgment and control made us irritable, easily enraged; we flared up constantly but were afraid to let go of our feelings. We distrusted ourselves and each other, as if under the surface something terrible might be lurking. We communicated obliquely, often with sarcasm. Treachery was not uncommon among us, as I had learned early. In general we lived in an atmosphere of muted, barely contained rage.

We children each handled our rage somewhat differently. When he was little, Erik used to lose his temper, but as he got older he learned better control. Like our mother, he was good at distance; when he was around me I could practically feel him leaning away. "What do *you* want?" he would say, and it wasn't a question; it was a command: Shut up and go away.

Arno could be as frightening as my father. He had the same general look, like a volcano about to blow, and as little patience. Once a small cousin was staying with us and everyone else had gone off somewhere, leaving Arno in charge of me and the cousin, who was still using a potty. Arno was raking leaves and carrying enormous sacksful down to the back yard to burn. Every time he walked past the back of the house, where there was a toilet in its own little room next to the woodbin, the cousin would whine that he had to pee. Arno's sack, in those pre-plastic-leaf-bag days, was a tarpaulin gathered and tied at the corners, impossible to put down without losing leaves and making a mess. He had the option of doing that, or of ignoring my cousin's whines and continuing on down to the back to dump his load, risking being responsible for an accident before he could get back up the hill.

The constant repetition of this choice wore on Arno. I watched his rage rise over the course of the afternoon, fascinated to see what he might do to the cousin if it erupted. But he kept himself under control. That was even more frightening. When he stopped to help the toddler, his movements were slow and exaggerated. He spoke very deliberately, through clenched teeth, in a tone just this side of hysteria. My cousin was terrified. I was silent. I was a little afraid Arno might turn on me, but I couldn't tear myself away. My cousin was asking for attention, something I had learned very early never to do. I think I felt awed that he dared and, meanly, self-righteous about the fact that, while he was getting what he wanted, he was being punished with the blast of Arno's mood.

MY FATHER liked to test people. One summer when I was very small, when we were living in Fort Wayne, I drove down with my parents to visit two of my brothers at summer camp. I was at an age when nobody pays any attention to you, so you can stand around and stare at almost anything that's going on. I watched my father while he went into the tent in which one of my brothers slept. It was an old army tent: heavy, coarse, olive-drab canvas with high straight sides and a peaked top. The flaps were open at each end so you could see the wooden floor with cots and little lockers lined up on either side. My father stepped up to my brother's cot, put his hand in the side pocket of his pants, and pulled out a quarter. He balanced it on a little platform he made by wedging his right thumbnail into the angle between the first and second joints of his right index finger, just like you do when you shoot marbles. He snapped his right thumb smartly upward and the coin arced toward the canvas ceiling, its rim angling until, at apogee, it turned over, like a diver doing a back flip, and fell to hit the bed at a steep slant. It didn't bounce; just collapsed and lay on the brown blanket.

My father grunted, picked up the quarter. "You'd never pass an Army inspection," he told my mortified brother.

His tests for me and my mother were different, less finite. Women didn't have to know how to make a bed well enough so the inspecting officer could bounce a quarter on it. Women's bedmaking was home stuff; it didn't count in the world of men. My father's test for my mother and me was that we should make no demands on him. But of course my mother had four children and a house to look after; she had to make demands.

Before the war, she had been compliant enough, moving whenever necessary, putting up with rented and temporary houses, investing very little of herself in any of them. If there was political friction, it was muted; what with Roosevelt and the New Deal, the times were sympathetic to socialists. Government agencies like the WPA suggested a satisfying blend of the aesthetic and political. Paul Robeson, who was pro-Communist and had visited Russia, recorded *Ballad for Americans* in 1939; at some point, perhaps during the war when Russia was our ally, my mother acquired the album.

Even though my mother was a very competent person, my father had always been able to devastate her. But during the war, she spent two or three years making her own decisions, without my father around all the time to second-guess her. I think she acquired a little more confidence in her own judgment, although she was still nervous.

And then in St. Davids, after sixteen years of moving at the whim of the railroad, she came alive to her surroundings, became committed to her life. She was prepared, now, to risk herself: she became engaged by her domestic projects, by her committees, by my education. She had found her own turf, at last; I think she believed that she would finally achieve her mother's serenity.

My father was oblivious to all this. He certainly didn't recognize any territory as my mother's; in his view she inhabited, on suffrance, a patch of his turf. In effect, she belonged to him, and her duty was to live for his convenience. He naturally expected her old compliance.

Eventually they quarreled. I had no memory of previous arguments, because for so much of my conscious life my father had been away. But at some point in St. Davids I began to perceive that the tension between them would build until they were webbed in it, more oblivious to the rest of us than usual. Gradually, it seemed to me, their antagonism became their relationship.

Out in the world, the red tide was rising; Americans were being investigated and indicted, books were being banned, even Truman—a Democrat!—was sending military aid to shore up Greece against the Commies. My father, a good Republican, repudiated his ex-colleagues of the Russian army and became a rabid anti-Communist. My mother was interested in Henry Wallace, founder of the Progressive Party, adherent of the principles of the United Nations charter. My father said Wallace was a Communist—or, at the very least, a fellow-traveler, a Commie dupe.

The Cold War raged inside our house. The fact that Paul Robeson had been to Russia before the war was now damning; so was the fact that he supported Henry Wallace. To my father, it all added up; Robeson was a Communist. Everybody knew it. At some point, after the founding of the Progressive Party in 1947, or maybe after the notorious Peekskill concerts in the summer of '49, when patriotic citizens got together to stone the Commies—what did the reds expect, my father asked rhetorically, when they invited Paul Robeson to sing propaganda songs?—the Robeson album disappeared from our house.

Inevitably at some point my father intimated that my mother might herself be a dupe, a fellow-traveler. Her ideas were just the thin end of the wedge; you could no more be a little bit Communist than you could be a little bit pregnant.

My father might have been worried about his job: the Pennsylvania Railroad was rock-ribbed Republican, WASP through and through. He may have feared he was potentially suspect for having worked so closely with the Russians during the war, although he never got rid of the medal they had given him. Nor did he throw out my mother's copy of Nicholas Berdyaev's *Origins of Russian Communism,* which surely would have been incriminating if the feds had turned up at our house. But he hammered away at my mother to change her views and quit the League of Women Voters, whose political neutrality he thought was the sure sign of a Communist-front organization.

Nobody acknowledged their quarrel: it went on after dinner, after we children had left the dining room; low-voiced, bitter exchanges, catercorner across the table between my father's chair at the head and my mother's to his left, while they drank their black coffee and liqueur and she chain-smoked Camels, staining yellow the top joints of the first two fingers of her right hand. They kept it up in the kitchen, right under my bedroom, while she washed and he dried, or he paced up and down and smoked his pipe furiously.

My father demanded to know about the Frenchwoman

who was giving me language lessons. My mother invited her
to dinner. The Frenchwoman and my father talked some
politics and reviewed their wartime experiences. She had
lived through the Occupation, developing a healthy dislike
of Fascists. Socialism offered the only hope for a peaceful
future, she thought; didn't he agree? On his mettle, trying
to be urbane and charming, he was noncommittal.

During dessert the Frenchwoman offered to read our
fortunes in coffee grounds or tea leaves. Arno, obviously
entranced, leaped to the challenge; the Frenchwoman
swirled grounds around in his cup, read him a flattering
future, fluttered her eyelashes at him. He blushed.

The upshot was, of course, that my father didn't like the
Frenchwoman's politics, and my mother had to tell me I
couldn't have any more French lessons.

I couldn't see what politics had to do with my learning to
write *la plume de ma tante;* I was angry that the lessons had
been taken away from me. But I was more afraid of my
father's anger—and of my mother's potential anger at me for
getting her into trouble with my father. All this made me
feel relieved, on the whole, that the source of provocation
had been removed. I missed the French teacher, though—
missed the glamour of her, the sense of a grown woman who
had a life of her own. And of course I missed the feeling of
being real that the French lessons had given me.

I didn't realize that my father was using me to get at my
mother. I may have sensed it, on some level, but I couldn't
have articulated it. My mother must have known it, though.
It was as though he felt her sheer existence diminished him,

so that any power she had, even just to do something for me, was pure threat.

The Cold War period was thoroughly misogynist; one paranoia matched the other. On the radio, George was putting down Gracie, while in Thurber's cartoons, much admired by my father, little men were overwhelmed by giant, threatening wives, and in novels written by men (the only kind that were taken seriously) wives were bitchy, frigid creatures who refused to go down on their long-suffering husbands. It was pure doublethink: women were silly and incompetent, but they could emasculate men as easily as godless Communists could infiltrate American Christian Republican minds—which is to say, as easily as a good pitcher could slip a curve ball past a hapless batter.

My father's misogyny was equally general and all-encompassing. I think he finally came to perceive my mother as something very like godless Communism, against which he would defend his American Christian Republican maleness by any means he found.

My mother shrank under his assault. He was passing judgment on her, and she was passing judgment on herself. She smoked more and talked less, and retreated farther into her old refuge, perfectionism. Only a few years before, she had bent her ferocious will to perfection on me and my body, but now I was too old for that. Under the circumstances, escaping into external perfection, into brief moments of beauty, was useless. To get through everyday life among the men, to banish the rage and the sweating anxiety at the center of herself, she yearned to *be* perfect, the way I yearned to be someone else.

Maybe that was why she had never been able to trust herself to her art. The forms she created were slender bridges over chaos; she couldn't convince herself that they would hold her. She relied on the careful suburban rules of life that make perfection seem tantalizingly possible—or, rather, make it easy to envision an accumulation of small, easily attainable perfections—the perfect pan of sticky buns, the perfect dining room, the perfect party, the perfect meeting—that will add up to a perfect life.

As a perfect wife, my mother applied all the ruthlessness she might have used as an artist in the service of her work to herself and her housekeeping. She bought the right clothes for the wife of a rising executive, and she dressed impeccably for every occasion. She entertained my father's colleagues and boss. She made his favorite pies and cakes, his waffles, his roasts, his jams. She made sure his boxer shorts were ironed the way he liked them. She kept the house immaculate. But once her first expansionist burst of energy had abated, once the quarrel started, there wasn't any joy in all this; there was only the compulsion of a terrible need. Her mood was grim; anxiety was overwhelming her. Against it, she was using perfectionism the way other people use alcohol or cocaine; it was a drug, and she was an addict.

AS FAR as my father was concerned, money was probably the penultimate betrayal. My parents had argued about money from the start; my aunt remembered raised voices and slammed doors starting early in the marriage. Something to do with insurance. My father was putting a lot of money into policies, while continually criticizing my mother's management of household expenses. He gave her that money, so he naturally wanted to control the way she spent it.

Now we children were growing up—in the fall of '49, Arno went off to college. We all had more needs—for clothes, for food (sons arriving home after football practice might each drink a quart of milk and eat a leftover-meat sandwich before dinner), for gas for the prewar Studebaker. Frills like my French lessons cost money, too, which was probably another reason why my father stopped them. At the same time, he was making his investments in the house, and he had three more children to send to college.

Did he deal with my mother the same way he dealt with us children? Did he review her faults as he reviewed ours before he gave out our allowances on Sunday nights after dinner, and during his annual review to see whether we deserved raises? These were excruciating exercises in public criticism. My father saw them as open, democratic family councils, but to me, at least, they seemed entirely arbitrary; he was laying down his law, and there was no recourse. I would sit, waiting, head down, while he settled my brothers' hash, trying to guess by the amounts he awarded them what I might get, hoping he wouldn't spend too much time dissecting me, trying not to get my hopes up so I wouldn't be too disappointed. He wouldn't withhold your allowance if you hadn't come up to snuff, but he made you believe that he would if you were ever to step over some undefined line and behave *too* badly. It was a foregone conclusion that whatever he said we would accept, silently.

Anything we wanted that our allowances wouldn't cover was a problem. My father didn't like buying things for us, and he was a hard man to negotiate with. Hal, who had a paper route from the time he was quite young, preferred to buy his own guns and bicycles out of the money he earned.

When I was seven, I desperately wanted a bicycle. My friend Barbara, the minister's daughter, had just received from her father a brand-new Schwinn, full-size, all shining maroon and chrome. My mother, who thought I wandered too much already, wasn't happy about providing me with the means for even greater mobility, but my father at length announced that I could have a bicycle if I paid for part of it out of my allowance. He would withhold some fraction of it for however many weeks or months it took to pay off my share. I think I was getting a quarter a week, so the bike would have to be very cheap, in fact secondhand. As it happened, my father knew of such a bike, three-quarter size, for sale at the gas station down toward Radnor Station. They wanted seven dollars for it. It was a boy's bike, its ancient frame pitted and rusty. My father persuaded the sellers to throw in a paint job, so that by the time I actually got it even the handlebars were a light matte blue.

I rode all over the neighborhood on that bike, next to Barbara on her shiny new Schwinn. I rode faster than she did, to prove that even though my bike was smaller and secondhand, it was just as good; better, even. I was trying to outride my feelings.

Was it from his mother that my father acquired the fixed

notion that money was love and vice versa, and that if you
gave any of either away you lost it forever, so the trick was to
sell everything for as much cash as you could demand? If he
was telling me I wasn't worth a whole lot in the way of either
money or love, he must have told my mother the same thing,
over and over again. I remember how he would pause and
lean back in his chair, as if he were deciding just how he was
going to attack, just what he was going to take away. Then he
would lean forward and look at you with his steely gangster
eyes.

I doubt that my mother ever asked for any of the new
consumer goods beginning to flood the market—a dish-
washer, a second car, a TV set—although she might very
well have wanted, and certainly could have put to good use,
a freezer and clothes dryer. But she did want to give me the
accomplishments she thought a young lady ought to have.

She bought the old upright piano when I was eight, the
spring of the year before she killed herself, and told my
father she wanted me to have lessons. He looked at her over
the dinner table, and then at me, standing next to her,
holding my breath—I wanted those lessons more than anything. He narrowed his gaze and delivered his judgment:
the piano was a waste of money. (She hadn't consulted him
about buying it, knowing in advance that he wouldn't approve, and he was furious.)

Lessons would be a waste of time; he didn't intend to let
me ruin his peace with scales and sour notes and general
incompetence. He doubted that I would ever keep it up long
enough to be any good at it, anyway; he knew my capacity
for hard work, and he didn't think much of it. Besides,

unlike my oldest brother, who had an excellent voice, I had never displayed the slightest iota of musical talent.

I suppose the fact that my father was tone deaf—something I didn't realize until I was much older—meant that he had no feeling at all for music. But the meanness of his eyes and words paralyzed me with the dilemma of whether I *deserved* that piano, those lessons, or not. The issue expands, becomes a cosmic one; how good do you have to be before you're good enough to be able to learn how to do something? Or even, merely, to have something? Or be someone?

It's an unanswerable conundrum. My mother, finally, could only slice through it, violently.

ELEVEN

Hiroshima,
Mon Amour

DURING THE quarrel family life went on, with, as always, the pretense that nothing was out of order. Summers were always the best time for me, because my brothers and I spent our days at Martin's Dam, a swimming club on a small lake. Our first summer I started in the baby pool, a shallow, fenced-in corral between the high-dive platform and a dock. Hal taught me to lift my feet off the bottom and kick, trusting the water to hold me up. I danced fearfully on one leg for a week, and then, all at once, learned the miraculous lesson. By the end of the summer I had won a race and graduated to the immensity of the lake, where in the summers that followed my friends and I would play king of the raft, or dive, or sun ourselves in heaps on the docks and rafts until some big boys came along and pushed us into the water.

In the late afternoons, my mother would often drive over to pick us up. Sometimes she would persuade my father to come for a swim and, occasionally, a picnic supper. My mother always swam a lap all the way around the lake in her strong, slow crawl. My father would swim out to a raft, heave himself up and sit, puffing. When my mother had almost finished her lap he would dive in, swamping the raft, and swim back with her.

After supper I would swing far out over the water on a thick, knotted rope that hung from an overhanging tree branch. That was the closest thing to eternity I knew, to swing out into the mystery of evening and drop into the warm, dark, slithery water. When I came up I was part of the shadowy, silent world of lake and trees, under a high, pale sky. On the shore, in near darkness, my mother sat with my father at the picnic table, immersed in one of their endless discussions. Fireflies danced around the still glow of her cigarette.

MY FATHER was transferred to New York, to run the northern division of the railroad from Penn Station, the biggest and busiest in the system. He wasn't willing to endure a four-hour commute every day, so he stayed in New York and came home on weekends. He wanted to move us to New Jersey so he could come home every night.

My mother meant to stay in St. Davids. She told my father she would never leave that house.

My father could not comprehend how a house could mean that much to anyone. Penn Station would make him. It was the last test before he would be called back to Philadelphia to a vice president's office. And in any case, they had been nomads their whole marriage; what difference would one more move make?

But of course, it wasn't just a house. It was her whole identity. The crowning statement of her life, the form into which she had chosen to put all her art.

If my father had any inkling of this, he was unmoved. He found a big stucco house in Cranford, New Jersey, on the bank of the Rahway River, and bought it.

AS FAR as I know, this was the first time my mother had really resisted my father. I think she had always seen in him the father who charmed and withheld, teased and denied, and whom she wanted above all to please. I think she never stopped seeing him like that, even as she dug in her heels. (I can understand that. Until long after I was grown and he had died I never stopped fantasizing that I could, and somehow would, please him myself; to have given up would have been to admit that I was a hopeless case, a failure, terminally incapable of pleasing the most powerful and seductive man in my life. After my mother killed herself, of course, that need to please took on shades of desperation: what would be the penalty if I failed?) So it was inevitable that the more he turned on her, the more she would turn on herself, for not being perfect enough to stop him.

In the face of my mother's resistance, I think my father somehow felt himself in danger of sinking back into shamed and impotent boyhood—my mother standing in for his mother, who had had the power to banish him from her house and force him to live and work alone in a strange town. This time he had to defeat her.

My mother was desperate and cold; my father was demanding and cold. The shit congealed inside both of them, but they held onto it. They were alike in that; neither could let anything go.

In our family, no one recognized the existence of the other, the life of the other: a wife was part of her husband, a child was part of her mother. Any little gesture of independent activity was subversive; separation was tantamount to revolt. We dreamed the dream of total control, a pornographer's dream, and our love was a pornographer's love, the manipulation of a fantasy person with no life of her own. In Fort Wayne, when I was very small, that had been my mother's dream of me; it remained, perhaps, her dream of herself. It was certainly my father's dream of my mother and me, his dream of women. In Fort Wayne he had collaborated with my mother against me, helped her sabotage my body, sticking his finger in to see whether I was willfully withholding what she had commanded me to release, then helping to hold me down for the enema that invariably followed. Against her, he would be as ruthless as he had been with her against me.

Men who love this way will tell their wives they're worthless; if they're physically as well as emotionally violent, they'll beat them. Yet they have to have them. They will destroy a wife rather than lose her, but if they keep her they will destroy her anyway.

THE TENSION in the household was exquisite: my father and mother locked in mortal combat, myself drawn, moth to candle, to their tight circle of energy. Nothing outside that deadly circle seemed real to me. Together, completely absorbed in their mutual hatred, they were even more fascinating than my mother alone had been in Fort Wayne, sitting at her desk or standing in the kitchen with her back turned. I couldn't take my eyes off her then; I couldn't keep away from the two of them now. I wanted to be there in case they stopped arguing, and I wanted to be there in case he suddenly reached across the table and grabbed her by the throat. I never saw it happen; I only heard it in his voice.

I wanted to help her, but there wasn't anything I could do. She seemed so alone. My father had, implicitly, the whole male world and a good part of the female one at his back, cheering him on. Had his job to go to each day, where a secretary and other office underlings were obsequious, and all the train crews were subject to his command. His place near the top of the company ladder was secure, and an even higher rung beckoned.

Where did my mother go for rest and rehabilitation, for support? The League of Women Voters? I don't think she ever would have admitted a private problem into that carefully crafted public world. Her women friends? She threw out her line to her future daughter-in-law's mother, but didn't get a nibble. Probably it was the same with any other women friends she spoke to. Who could reach out in support, in understanding? Each woman was isolated within her marriage, felt completely responsible for its success. If she had problems—and who didn't?—she couldn't afford to admit them.

I don't know whether my mother ever talked to her own mother; could the ever-resourceful Emma have imagined such despair? I think she would have told my mother to do what she must, but I don't think my mother could have admitted failure to her — admitted that, after she had gambled for her mother's prizes, waited all those years for a house of her own, the marriage on which the whole thing depended was falling apart.

Her only retreat was into her gardens, her cooking, her baking of bread and cakes and pies — all she had gotten from her own mother as a girl, all she could still share with her. Gardens and cooking were her pipelines to the magic stuff of which women are supposed to be made, the inexhaustible stuff with which they feed men.

However hard she tried, she couldn't go into serene withdrawal, as her own mother could. When Emma sat still, she seemed filled with the riches of a benign universe. But her solution to problems had shut my mother out; when my mother emulated her, she went into a depression, as she had in Fort Wayne, sitting in the puny backyard in the afternoon sun. As she did now, more and more. It was as though at the center of her being she felt only a void, a knot of darkness, and when she sat still she lost herself in it. Doing things, she came alive, might still be perfect; sitting still, she was like the hawk chained in her father's studio, beating her wings, helpless to rise.

And she had picked a man, my father, who swallowed her up; demanded absolutely and implacably all her resources, but gave her back nothing. She had found a man with a grudge against women, in a world designed to encourage men to blame women for their own difficulties, for not smoothing their way and healing all their hurts, for not really being the all-powerful goddesses they feared them to be, and so being unable to solve all their problems and make the world safe for a democracy in which each man was king.

I WANTED to get my mother a birthday present that would please her. I knew she liked silver. She had this beautiful antique Norwegian silverware, enormous hand-cut dinner forks engraved with Christian names and dates, like AGNES 1845. As if a fork had been made for each child born in the family and passed along with the accumulation of generations.

Things ordered from cereal boxtops had a lot of power for me, because in my earliest memories my brothers had played with magic rings and such that they had ordered with boxtop coupons. Some boxtop offered a set of four genuine silver-plated teaspoons, for an amount of money I had saved up from my allowance. My mother was by this time far gone in depression, sitting in her place at the table, hardly speaking. I wanted to get her blessing on the idea of this present before I clipped the coupon, so I showed her the picture of the spoons and asked her whether she liked them. She said yes, so I sent away for them. When I gave them to her, I think she made an effort to respond, but I could tell she was already someplace farther away than her chair at the table.

We had a white canvas navy-surplus hammock in the side yard, strung between two hemlock trees, that I had more or less taken over for horse, house, boat, and anything else that suggested itself. I remember one unusually warm day not long before my mother killed herself, when I tried to interest her in playing with me and a doll in the hammock. I remember she actually came over and sat next to me on the edge of the hammock. I was holding the doll, and my mother was staring off somewhere. It was frightening to have her body next to me on the hammock, to have her gentle and reasonable, not getting mad at me for making demands on her, willing to let me seat her right next to me, and know she wasn't really there at all.

She had this sweet reasonableness at the end; it was as though she had decided that if my father wanted compliance she would go through the motions, while she was actually out searching for her own form of violence, some kind of speech that would give my father a message he couldn't ignore.

Because she could not in reality speak to him (since he would not listen), because she could neither exist in his house nor get a divorce, because she had decided there was no place in the real world where she could exist, she decided to resort to a symbolic act that turned out to be the most violent reality of all: death.

TWENTY YEARS before, when my father had seemed to share her pleasure in art, she had believed he was sensitive to her, aware of her. She had mistaken his sensuality for generosity, his narcissism for concern.

She was now free of those illusions.

They were still sleeping in the same bed. My father's appetite for food, for drink, for sex, was as hearty as ever.

His sensuality was heavy, insistent; she fed him, but she had given up everything that might have fed her. And what she had not given up he had taken away.

If he still aroused her sexually, she may increasingly have felt her appetite as gross, shameful. Or she may have lost interest in him. Either way, sex, that can be redemptive, restoring the self by centering it within the feeling body, would instead have isolated her more and more from herself.

She must have felt a terrible self-disgust, and she must have been afraid. She was forty-four; middle-aged in those days. The next step would be menopause; where would she find a new man? How could she start over, when she had only just reached her goal?

She was tired. She was very depressed. She had stopped eating, was thin enough to lie on the ironing board in front of the oven. She felt a great desire to rest.

She made her decision with immense gravity and consideration, and with an artist's desire to satisfy all the requirements of a commission: the aesthetic demands of the space, the moral and economic demands of the sponsor, the artist's need to communicate something of what she felt and perceived. Her act was like a fifteenth-century painting in which the sponsor and his family kneel along the bottom edge, the husband with his sons behind him on one side, the wife with her daughter behind her on the other, facing each other across the plane of the picture. Their bodies define the foreground; behind them, the artist is free to fill the space with the new glories of perspective. Only my mother was a modern artist; she was interested in destroying both perspective and its twin, time.

TWELVE

The Book of
Ezekiel

AFTER THE funeral, we went ahead and made the move
to Cranford that had driven my mother to kill herself.
She had made good her assertion, and now my father was
going to cancel out her act.

He, my brothers and aunt packed up our things. I was
staying with my friend Judy Marshall and getting no information about what was happening, but naturally I was
curious. One day, out playing with my friend Theresa, I
burst into the scrubbed but still scarred kitchen, where my
father and Hal were crating dishes. "You shouldn't be in
here!" my father said, loudly and abruptly. For the second
time in as many weeks I stopped in my tracks, hesitated,
then backed out of the kitchen. It felt very strange to be
summarily barred from one of the places where I had been
closest to my mother. My father's words took on a larger

significance than the immediate situation, as if they were a cosmic message beamed exclusively at me.

The moving truck was sent on ahead, and one morning we got in the car and drove to New Jersey. We didn't have a cat carrier, so Hal held the terrified animal on his lap, and it peed on him. When we got to the new house the cat, disoriented but gamely trying to play by the usual rules, peed in the fireplace. Hal was by this time furious, and he put the cat outside. We never saw it again. I thought it had gotten the message that it shouldn't be there and had slunk off in shame.

Some other family might have drawn together in Cranford that summer after the suicide, but we didn't. How could we, when our only centripetal force was gone? We were each immersed in our own shock, each planning an escape. Nothing had prepared us to deal with a suicide; we wanted to deny all knowledge of it.

The tone of my postsuicide relationship with my father had been set the day after we discovered my mother's body, when he arrived from New York. Having been up all night, I was resting in bed at the Irish Magistrate's house, reading a comic book. I remember I was wearing my red cowboy shirt with the white fringe. The door opened and my father's face appeared, scowling. He looked at me for a minute and said, "Are you all right?" "Yes," I said, intensely uncomfortable. He withdrew, still scowling.

I was soon sent to stay with the Marshalls. There nobody bothered me, and I did my best to immerse myself in a running fantasy of living in prehistoric times. I also made small talk and had the odd pillow fight with Judy, whose room I shared, listened to Spike Jones records and practiced jacks, which had never before interested me but the mindless, unvarying ritual of which I now found soothing. I remember I was sitting on the dining-room floor in the sun playing jacks by myself when my aunt, my mother's sister-in-law, came in. She squatted down facing me and asked, "Do you want to go to your mother's funeral?"

I immediately felt claustrophobic. Somehow I knew she was going to be cremated, and I could not have said which image was worse; my mother sealed in a blunt box, or body and box being burned to ash. For all I knew, the coffin would be open during the funeral, and I would have to look at her dreadful stillness one more time.

So I whispered, "no," and my aunt stood up and left.

As far as I was concerned, that was pretty much the extent of family discussion about my mother's suicide. There was the moment when I overheard my father, overcome by grief, rushing through the Cranford house calling my mother's name. But of course I could never speak of this incident. It remained in my head, an image, indistinguishable from a fantasy to anyone who might be looking in from outside, and denied by everything else that was happening in the household.

What was happening was a pretense of everyday life. Erik and Hal took charge of laundry and cooking, the latter consisting mainly of hamburgers, hot dogs (Hal liked them split and fried; Erik boiled them) or frozen chicken pot pies, with frozen french fries and frozen spinach or string beans. I stood around and watched. I passionately wanted to take charge of the cooking and help with the laundry; it seemed to me that as my mother's daughter I ought to be carrying on her duties, taking her place in the household. But of course I never mentioned this fantasy, and it never occurred to my brothers to ask me to help them.

Eventually my father found a housekeeper who stayed each day to put supper on the table. Her kitchen was completely out of bounds, and I soon got into trouble with her. I remember one day coming out of the kitchen (she was upstairs cleaning) with a box of marshmallows, intending to ask her whether it was all right if I ate one. Erik and Hal were in the hall by the stairwell; the minute they saw me they yelled upstairs, "Signe's eating marshmallows!" (I probably did have my hand in the box, at least.) The housekeeper sent me to my room. I could not bear the injustice of this punishment, so I hid in the closet and refused to come out.

Once we had the housekeeper, my father seldom came home except to sleep; running Penn Station absorbed him so completely that he often worked Sundays as well as Saturdays. I finished out the fourth grade in a new school, where they were studying ancient history. For some reason, they were still on Egypt, and I became fascinated by mummies. I looked up the subject in our Encyclopedia Britannica, 11th edition, and studied the details of the process of mummification. Rich people had their innards taken out and preserved separately; really important guts might be given their own funeral urn. The bodies were soaked in a big vat of aromatic resins and other preservatives that somehow immortalized the finger- and toenails too. Poor people were slung with hooks into a common vat, innards and all.

My father was pleased by my interest, and one Sunday took us to see the mummies at the Metropolitan Museum in New York City. But I was horrified by the stone sarcophagi and the tightly wrapped, body-shaped packages with their painted face masks. I had not realized that preservation was preparation for burial; I thought it had something to do with reversing death. The preserved person might walk into the house any day and start fixing lunch.

Most students walked home for lunch, so the school didn't serve food. For a while, I ate a tuna-fish sandwich at the counter in a drugstore where a number of teachers had lunch. I took to bringing my volume of the Encyclopedia Britannica to prop up on the counter in front of me; I had discovered the consolations of precocity, the soothing balm of adult admiration. I did make one close friend at school, and spent a fair amount of time at her house. To some extent I also followed my old pattern of making the rounds of the neighborhood, becoming welcome in different houses and getting to know most of the kids. As in St. Davids, there were a lot of big houses with lawns, through and over which a tide of children continually ebbed and flowed, playing giant steps on the sidewalk in front of the house next door, or hide and seek in our side yard that had the huge copper beech. Sometimes I hung out with some twelve-year-old girls, who for some reason tolerated me at their rituals of sewing, making snacks and desserts, reading magazines, and examining each other for signs of breast development. When I was with other kids, it sometimes felt as though nothing had ever happened. I was floating through a dreamy landscape, a never-never land of sweet trivialities.

I suppose my father and brothers were doing the same thing, focusing on small daily activities to keep their minds off the ungraspable hugeness of what had happened. We had no words for feelings, but even if we had, I would not have been able to use them. The circuits in my brain were jammed.

But what I felt I have gone on feeling, in dreamscapes far removed from that one. I was numb with terror at my mother's apocalyptic rage. The explosion had cut loose, uprooted, destroyed all the landmarks, all the solid corners that had held my universe together. Called everything into question. Behind the terror I felt very small and very empty, completely inadequate to deal with such an immensity. Above all, I felt intense shame, for myself and for her, and a terrible dread. She had made a huge mess and implicated me. Sooner or later, I would have to pay for it.

I stopped saying my prayers. I had always assumed God was a distant, angry judge, like my father; I had said my prayers every night, but it had never occurred to me to turn to him for consolation. Now it seemed safer to avoid him altogether. Since I was terrified of what was inside me, I tried to empty myself of awareness.

Our back yard was bordered by the Rahway River, actually a fair-sized creek that ran through the town, out past the yards of apartment buildings and houses and, eventually, through a swamp and a woods. An old green canvas kayak had come with our house, and I learned to paddle it. As the weather grew warmer, I began spending weekend afternoons and then whole summer days on the creek. I found a kind of peace there, floating along, exploring, taking in the landscape, thinking of nothing in particular. One day I found spent shotgun shells eddying in the weeds at the edge of the swamp and feared violence, but saw no other signs of it.

I was, just, still young enough to lose myself in make-believe. On the river I began to invent elaborate plots involving people who might live in the houses I passed. In the woods, where I often walked all day when I wasn't kayaking, I became an Indian, an eighteenth-century brave out of James Fenimore Cooper; an aristocrat of the forest, treading silently on the balls of my feet. I was an invincible stoic, unafraid of hunger, thirst, or torture, and, in my natural element, invisible to the crude, clumsy, noisy whites. I could sneak up and scalp one of them any time, then melt back into the landscape.

I had always read as much as I could, but books and magazines now became a crucial escape. I read indiscriminately and lived inside plots: *Ivanhoe, The Bobbsey Twins, The Last of the Mohicans*. I read magazines cover to cover, including the tiny print in the ads on the back pages of women's magazines, offering cures for the heartbreak of psoriasis or the tragedy of lordosis, or revelation of the secrets of the Rosicrucians. I tried to fit my consciousness completely within the thin black lines around those ads; I didn't want any rough edges of myself to overlap the print.

I was trying to invent a new self, one that would be like something somebody else had already written so I would know I was OK. I wasn't supposed to be there, but I had to hang on to myself somehow. I wanted my thoughts to match the text some copy editor had already approved — except I didn't know about copy editors yet, so I thought of someone something like God, who decided what to print, what to lay out there so people could see it. I thought a god-editor would never print the bad stuff, the mistakes, anything that might do some harm.

Women's magazines were written for the kind of woman I was supposed to grow up to be, but I couldn't recognize my own situation in any of them. Nobody I knew had ever had lordosis, and the problems that seemed so urgent to the people quoted in the articles, that were discussed so earnestly by the psychiatrists in their columns, seemed unreal. But my mother had subscribed to those magazines, so I thought that if I read them I could perhaps figure out how to be the kind of person who would not have alarmed or angered her, much less have done her in.

What I wanted was not to have killed my mother, and not to be accessible to anyone, like my father, who might also have done it or who was in a position to judge that I had. Under no circumstances could I be spontaneously myself. I was very stern about editing the connecting links between feeling, memory, perception, and idea, and between idea and speech or idea and action. Editing and abridging impulses before translating them into action is a normal process of socialization, but I was extreme. I wanted to cut the links altogether; it was a matter of life and death. If I should for one minute forget myself, expose myself, I would be vulnerable to my mother's rage, or my father's, or my own.

MY FATHER knew what I had no idea of yet, that my mother had mocked him with her death. Had said, *See, this is what I think of the bargain I've made with you; death is a better place for me than your house.*

God knows what my brothers knew, or thought. That summer Arno was already halfway out of the family into his own life. Hal was in the flower of his adolescence, a stocky, black-haired, muscular sixteen-year-old in skin-tight button-fly Levis, poised to make his own move but still partly held by the family. Erik was a gawky, half-grown fourteen-year-old with tightly curled blond hair he disliked and a voice that still cracked. He was my hated rival and sometime playmate, still held in the family grip but lightly, the centrifuge already spinning him outward.

I was caught. The suicide had blasted all my accommodations to smithereens. All the compromises I had managed to make between my mother's conscience and my own needs—between her demand for absolute perfection and my need to move around a bit, rub up against other people, get my clothes dirty and my hands scratched—were suspect; seemed tawdry and unworthy. The whole miserable pile of deals and evasions collapsed on me, leaving me dazed and furtive, my previous acts of independence and individuality reduced to the pilfering of a petty thief. Anything I took for my own life now would be stealing from her.

I could no longer sneak away, because my mother's view was no longer confined to the angles commanded by the front and side windows of her bedroom. Now she sat next to God and saw everything.

IN CRANFORD my bedroom was right next to my father's, on one side of the big hall upstairs; Erik and Hal had rooms off a short connecting back hall, with its own door that they could shut whenever they liked. My father usually came into my room in the mornings to wake me up for school before he left for work. I would wake up, and he would be standing in the doorway, a dark shape in a dark suit. Or he would be standing right by my bed, looking down at me.

I began to have trouble sleeping. I remember sitting on my bed looking at the photographs in an article in *Look* about life in a prison. Everything seemed to be green, including the prisoners' clothes. It was as though the whole prison were deep under the sea, everyone swimming around in these huge tiers of cells. The cells had no doors, just bars in front, so the guards could swim by and stare in at the prisoners whenever they liked.

AT THE end of that summer, just before my birthday, Korea was heating up and President Truman seized the railroads to prevent a general strike. My father put on his Reserve Army colonel's uniform and went down to Baltimore to run the Baltimore & Ohio Railroad. Hal and Erik were sent as boarding students to the boys' school in the little southern Pennsylvania town where my aunt and uncle, my father's brother and his wife, lived. I was sent to live with the same aunt and uncle and start fifth grade in the local public school, my third in a year.

I had three boy cousins around the same ages as my brothers; two were day students at the boys' school, so there were still plenty of boys around. Having no daughter, my aunt's notions of dealing with a girl went straight back to her own girlhood. I wasn't willing to have any woman mother me, so I was cranky, difficult, and very unhappy. My aunt and uncle made no more connection between my emotional state and the suicide than anyone else in the family ever did; it couldn't have been easy for them to deal with me.

I did make a good friend in that antique town, and in the warm southern fall we played around the alleyways and back galleries of the eighteenth-century rowhouses. It was a town that seemed never to have had an explosion. I made a hopeful, sentimental connection with the sweet, peaceful permanence of the pretty brick and stone houses, thick trees breathing in the early evenings, the little wooden houses on the back streets, the front-galleried, two-story commercial buildings around the square with its ornate, cast-iron fountain.

One day in late September or early October I came home from school and my aunt handed me a letter from my father. She left me alone to read it. It said that my father had gotten married again, and I was to go down to Baltimore to live with them. My mother had been dead barely six months. I had a feeling this was going to be something else I would have to live up to.

WE WANT it all back. Want her standing at the counter in her proper kitchen, stirring cake batter and holding up the spoon to judge the consistency of the coating. Want the transformation, in the innocent oven, of the batter into cake.

Want to watch her plunge the clean broom straw into the
centers of the risen cake layers and draw it out clean both
times. Want her to set the two pans onto racks to cool to a
temperature mortals can stand. Want the bowl of her chocolate fudge icing, the secret of which died with her, on the
front of the stove, keeping soft with the heat from the oven.
Want to watch her slather the icing on thick with the long
narrow spatula designed for this purpose. Want her to carry
the cake into the dining room for the final act of the miracle.
Want to say the word *cake,* making the *ke* sound far back in
the mouth, right above the taste buds, like a swallow. Want
to see the cake cut, the fudge hardened now to a thick slab.
Want the revelation of the soft yellow heart of the cake.
Want the taste in the mouth. Want the final transformation
of the cake into ourselves, the body and blood of the family.

IN BALTIMORE my father had a huge office and a patient
black steward in a white coat who had to entertain me when
I visited. I got my first glimpse of the woman who was to be
my stepmother, rushing down the hall in a cotton dress,
white gloves, and picture hat. She had been a clerk for the
railroad; my father met her soon after he arrived in Baltimore. This was her first marriage, and she had just quit her
job. She was about the same age as my mother had been six
months before. My father was brusquely cheerful in his
army uniform.

My first night in the city we all slept in a hotel, in the same
room, they in a double bed and I in a fold-up cot right next
to it. I lay awake all night listening to snoring and traffic.

The next day we drove out to the little house my father had bought or rented in a small development on the outskirts of Baltimore.

The house looked strangely familiar; small front lawn with sapling, short front walk, small doorstep with cast-iron railing, white clapboard siding. Inside, I could have found every room blindfolded. Small center entrance hall, living room to the left, dining room to the right. Kitchen at the back, through the dining room. Upstairs, master bedroom at the front of the house, two smaller bedrooms at the back, on either side of the center hall.

It was a clone of our house in Fort Wayne during the Second World War, when my father had also been in uniform and we hadn't yet moved to St. Davids. The only difference was that in this version I was given the bedroom Arno and Hal had shared in Fort Wayne. The room I had shared with Erik after my father came home on leave and evicted me from my mother's bedroom would be the guest room, for any brothers home from school on vacations. For the duration I was to be an only child.

We seemed to have moved backward in time, or out of time altogether. It was as though not only the suicide but our whole previous life as a family had never happened. I was supposed to be some kind of giant newborn baby, this man and woman my parents, all of us innocents together.

I was a little bit sick to my stomach the whole time we lived in that house. Even so, I got fat. I discovered that if I sat still, things didn't shift around so much, and if I ate, I felt a lot less anxious. My stepmother encouraged me by going with me to buy jelly- and cream-filled doughnuts; there were no sticky buns in this incarnation.

I didn't start eating right away. There was a brief honeymoon between my stepmother and me when my father would take us both out to dinner and to movies. I remember riding back in the car one night, my father driving, my stepmother and I in the back seat, I suppose to encourage me to get closer. My stepmother had on a black shirtdress, black gloves, and a black straw picture hat. She was a tall, rawboned woman with long jet-black hair in a roll or bun at the back of her head. I was tired and leaned against her shoulder. She put her arm around me, and I tried to lean against her bosom, but I didn't quite fit. She held her torso stiffly against the unaccustomed weight, and I kept encountering a sharp, awkward angle of collarbone or rib. It was hard to get under her picture hat; I had to squeeze down and tilt my spine to an uncomfortable angle. After a while I gave up.

In fact, we fit in very few ways. My stepmother liked to see herself as an ex-flapper who instead of going to college had become a model and lived a fast-paced social life that included a blind date with Archie Leach (later known as Cary Grant). But when she had had a few drinks, which was frequently, she saw herself as a martyr, who as the oldest daughter of a lace-curtain Irish family had been forced to quit school and go to work so her younger sister and brother could finish. They both married early, so it had fallen to her to sacrifice her time and energy for the duration of her mother's long last illness. She was full of rage about these sins against her youth and promise, and she never let any of us forget them.

Not that I could have been easy for her to deal with. I wanted no mothering from her, either. Our relationship was somehow settled by a couple of huge fights, when I fled to my bedroom and slammed the door, reopening it only to put up a KEEP OUT! THIS MEANS YOU! sign. My stepmother finally took to her bed with a headache and asked me to bring her a glass of beer. I could not refuse an appeal for help, so I came out of my room. I had had no experience of beer and because it was hot out I put ice in it. Later, as I sat on the side of her bed, she told me about beer and its uses and occasions, and how someone in her family had once put ice into beer, and what everyone had said about it at the time. I was partially hooked; my mother's naps had been inviolate, and she had seldom talked to me about anything. My stepmother had the southerner's habit of talking in stories, and she seemed to have an inexhaustible supply of them; her continuous stream of words filled the gaps in our relationship, as it was designed to do.

She had an impulsive, childish sense of fun. When we went one day to the Washington Zoo she persuaded my father to buy me a hamster. We took it with us, in a jar with a bit of bedding in it and a perforated lid, up the Washington Monument, to a movie and, afterward, to Miller's, the big Baltimore seafood restaurant, where I was allowed to unscrew the lid so the hamster could run around the tablecloth. The waiter, whom my stepmother knew, brought it a little salad of grated carrot and lettuce on a saucer. Nothing like this would ever have happened with my mother.

My stepmother also did her best to help me out with
school projects; one night, when I needed to make a model
of a generic Greek temple (all elementary schools seemed to
be studying ancient history), she helped me approximate
one with bars of soap carved roughly into columns. We dyed
tissue paper with green food coloring and dried it out in the
oven, then cut it up fine for grass.

She was quite capable of winking at school rules. When
one of my succession of hamsters got loose during the school
day, she would phone me at school to tell me, and then tell
the principal there had been an accident at home and to let
me go early. Once, when I was in sixth grade, she took me
out of school for the day to watch the Yankees in the World
Series. We sat high up in the bleachers and she pointed out
tiny figures that were Joe DiMaggio and Casey Stengel.

But I was on the edge of outgrowing her ideas of what I
ought to enjoy, and she never stopped wanting me to be a
child. Although she talked a great deal to me, there was very
little I could actually say to her; most of what I really
thought or felt or found interesting was offensive to her
rigid Catholic and lower-middle-class notions of propriety.
This was brought home to me early on when my father took
us to a movie about Martin Luther. Not very far into the
movie, a fat priest began selling indulgences in the main
square of Mainz to anyone who could pay for them. My
stepmother became very agitated and then got up and left,
followed by my father. He soon returned and stayed with
me to watch Martin Luther get the Reformation under way.
Afterward, we found my stepmother in the car, smoking a
cigarette.

"I don't know how you could watch such a thing," she said angrily. "I've never seen such slander. Priests never did anything like that. I can't imagine how they got away with making that movie. I'm telling you, someone should have shot Martin Luther."

I soon realized that she had something else in common with my mother besides leaving school prematurely: an absolute insistence on fitting me into her scheme of things. Just as with my mother, maximum passivity on my part got the best results. So I sat around eating filled doughnuts and listening to her stories, which before very long began to acquire a certain sameness. It seemed to me that she talked in order not to say anything. I missed my mother's silence, which by contrast seemed infinitely wise and very fine.

IN BALTIMORE I had my first intimation of menstruation. In the spring, when we girls were wearing cotton circle skirts to school, a sixth-grader got her period one day without knowing it. We all saw brown spots on the back of her skirt. Everyone knew what they were, but no one had the courage to tell her. Boys pointed out the spots to each other; some of them sniggered. I felt sick; this was what it would be like. You couldn't control it; you would mess yourself and everyone would know.

In Baltimore I began to have recurring atom-bomb dreams. In the early fifties, all the schools had air-raid drills. When you hear that the Bomb is on its way, you crouch under your desk or in the hall, along the locker side away from the windows. You cover your eyes with one arm and your head with the other. You crouch into a ball to protect your vital organs. When the all-clear sounds, you open your eyes to the ashes of your world.

In my dreams I would open the door of the house in St. Davids after the Bomb. Everything would be ash-gray: the yard thick with ash, the charred trees holding up their blasted, leafless branches.

Or the Bomb would swoop down and pick me up from the front step of the Baltimore house and carry me away, up to the top of its trajectory. The Bomb and I would do a big, lazy loop in the blue sky and then head back down, straight as an arrow toward the house.

MY FATHER definitely had something in mind. Maybe not consciously; he was flying on automatic pilot, like the rest of us. But somewhere in his mind he decided that we were merely in exile from the promised land. In his little tract house, from which he went forth each day in his army uniform to give his all for another war effort, he was making his plans to return. We weren't starting a new life at all; we were preparing to step back into our previous one. There weren't going to be any more new events in our lives, just repetitions of the old familiar ones.

During the exile of the Jews in Egypt after the destruction of the first Temple, the Prophet Ezekiel wrote that God had punished the Israelites for their sins, but that God was going to forgive them and that he, Ezekiel, had been given a vision of the new Temple to be built when they returned to Jerusalem. The prophet provided a detailed plan for the

Second Temple and its religious life-to-be. He described the ritual for each day of the week and each holy day, the number and kinds of animals to be sacrificed as sin offerings, who could be priests and what they could and could not wear, and the number of cubits in the length, breadth, and height of every wall, courtyard, doorway, and altar inside and outside the Temple.

It is easy to imagine Ezekiel in Egypt among his demoralized people, feverishly writing his book at night by the light of a tiny wick in a bowl of oil. Obsessively going over and over every detail, elaborating it, spinning the masses of detail into a ritual that would cover every conceivable aspect of worship and life and thereby hold together, cubit by cubit, sacrifice by sacrifice, his own psyche and the collective psyche of his people. The Temple in the mind would never fall.

What my father had in mind wasn't religious ritual, but it had the same purpose, salvation, and he brought to it the same obsessive attention to repetition and detail. It would create for us a space out of time, in which, when everything and everyone was in the right place, and the priest was chanting the liturgy, and the congregation was responding with the right words, and the soothing performance of the same activities that had been performed exactly the same way the day before and the day before that had created the feeling of eternity, the second miracle would happen.

She would be alive and in our midst.

THIRTEEN

The Second Coming

So we reversed direction and, by degrees, returned to the house in which my mother had killed herself. Seduced by the ease of the self-deception, we had all been dreaming, in the various outposts of our exile, of the family in its golden age, before the suicide. It had a certain mad logic: If we returned to the place where we had once been happy, we would certainly be happy there again. Even my stepmother, eager to fit in, heard the stories, caught the mood, and embraced the collective fantasy.

To make the symmetry complete, we paused in Cranford for a year while my father returned to New York City and Penn Station. He, my stepmother, and I lived in a cramped, makeshift apartment on the top floor of someone else's house until my father found a house in yet another small development on the edge of town. And then one day, two and a half years after the suicide, we drove back from New Jersey to Pennsylvania, turned into the curving carriage drive, and stepped out of the car onto the step down which I had watched the fireman carry my mother's body.

Although I was twelve, I don't remember that arrival, nor anything about moving back into the house. I think the effect of it was to lengthen and deepen my shell shock. My earliest memory from that time is of a school assembly during which I fell in love with a boy who was onstage giving a slide show about his summer vacation among the ruins of classical Greece. I wanted to be anywhere but in our house. I felt it wasn't our house any longer; it had become a shrine to my mother.

We furnished it almost exactly as it had been before the suicide. My grandfather's paintings and my mother's woodcut went back up on the walls of the dining room. The Pennsylvania Dutch cupboard was set up against its wall and filled with my mother's Indian Tree china. My father's big wing chair was installed next to the fireplace in the living room, and his grandfather clock was returned to its place in the front hall. On the third floor, each brother returned to his room. (Arno's was furnished pro forma, because he had finished college and joined the Navy.)

There were a few differences. The big upstairs family room next to the bathroom was furnished with the dark, heavy, mahogany-veneer furniture my stepmother had brought with her from Baltimore, and she and my father moved in. The little back room that had been my bedroom became my father's study, its flowered wallpaper, scribbled over with crayons by the child who had occupied it in our

absence, making an odd background for his tall walnut
filing cabinet, his desk, his brass desk lamp with its green
glass shade, and his mahogany case of Keuffel & Esser
drafting tools, all brass and wood and ivory in their fitted
green-felt-lined pull-out trays.

In the front bedroom that had been my mother's and
father's, my mother's solid mahogany bed, bureau, and
dressing table were set in their appointed places. The difference was that my father was a room away with his new wife,
while I slept alone in my mother's bed. Between us, the
gaping hole of the double closet.

SHRINES AREN'T always a matter of honor or veneration;
they can be built to placate the dead, to stave off guilt, to
deny anger. My father might have had all three of the less
public motives in mind. By the time we moved back to St.
Davids, he knew that my mother had destroyed his career.
When he was transferred to New York, he had assumed that
when he returned to Philadelphia it would be as a vice
president. Had he not been rising steadily all these years?
Had not his private life been above reproach, himself beyond all doubt abstemious, upright, and faithful? But it was
scandal that brought him down, the scandal created by my
mother, the ripples of the explosion reaching all the way to
the Pennsylvania Railroad executive offices in Philadelphia.
His rival, a man against whom he had been competing for
years, got the job, and my father was shunted to a dead-end
job as director of research, where he spent the rest of his life
investigating things like options in new railroad cars. And

then, to add insult to injury, after his Korean War stint in Baltimore, which surely would have helped him win his coveted general's commission, the railroad had demanded that my father quit the Army Reserve while he was still only a lieutenant colonel. Naturally he had acquiesced. So by the time he was forty-eight he knew he had failed to achieve either of his lifelong goals.

He was a stubborn man. He would never admit he was wrong about anything. He may in part have wanted to placate my mother, but he wasn't going to forgive her for ruining his hopes and smashing the smooth surface of his life. Neither were his sons, who are as stubborn as he was. If my mother had been telling them something about the family and her relationship to it, they weren't listening. They weren't interested in guilt. At some point, collectively and unconsciously, they made a decision: We weren't all in this together. I was in it; they were clean.

Every family has its own version of events, designed to reassure it that no matter what happens, it will survive. As a child grows, she is supposed to learn the family version, to believe in it, to tell her own stories from its point of view, and above all to become the person the family version expects her to be. In St. Davids, I began to realize that there was a whole subtext that referred to my mother but was really about me—about my guilt.

Guilt can create the desire to expiate or the desire to deny, to hide, to cover up. The deniers usually find it necessary or convenient to blame someone else: a scapegoat. The expiators, and those who are too young or too weak to choose, become the scapegoats. I was a natural scapegoat; I had had plenty of practice already.

Many families have a scapegoat, although none will admit it. The scapegoat is the child who, having been declared to be the devil, or merely irredeemably bad or evil, is scalded or beaten to death, or crammed into a pot and put on a hot burner to learn how to be good. Or, more subtly, infused with a sense of her own unworthiness as compared to everyone around her. By taking on their sins, the scapegoat affirms the innocence of everyone else in the family.

A girl will often be chosen for the role, although if none is handy a boy will do. Both can have the devil in them, but the devil in the boy is indigenous, while the devil in the girl is performing a sexual act. That distinction lends passion to those who scapegoat girls; a girl can take on the sexual guilt of men and women alike.

When I was very small, I became the scapegoat because I was littlest, and because I was a girl. I was my mother's means of punishing herself. A scapegoat is essential for people like her, who have no way to come to terms with themselves, no ground for forgiveness. They are their own calamities, and when they cannot find a scapegoat, or when the scapegoat runs away, as I did, they may turn on themselves, as my mother finally did.

After the suicide, the scapegoat coat fit me like a second skin. My aunts had been telling me my mother was an angel. When an angel commits suicide, you can't get angry at her for leaving you, for throwing away her life and ruining yours. I believed I must have done something terribly wrong to provoke her rage, to make her reject me so completely. She had always been too good for me; now she was completely beyond my reach. I felt I would never find out who she was, much less live up to her. But I had to have *some* connection to her; she had been my mother.

There was a secret, perverse power in the scapegoat role, and power had been in short supply in my life. Guilt, after all, implies responsibility, and responsibility implies importance. I had always felt my mother was peculiarly my responsibility, starting way back in Fort Wayne when it had come to me that I caused all her reactions to me. I was willing to sacrifice myself to keep up that connection.

SOMEHOW I strike a deal with my father. His position is that he has never pressed anyone to move, never bought the house in Cranford, never moved into it. He has been sitting here with me the whole time, out on the porch on summer evenings before dinner, by the big coffee table I've made from an old wooden table I found in the basement. I've stripped the paint off, clamped and glued a huge split in the top, cut down the legs, and sanded and refinished it. It was something to do, and I have done it as well as any brother. On it rest two of my father's rum specials, made with a layer of honey in the bottom of a highball glass, two ounces of rum over ice, soda, and a sprig of mint from the bed at the end of the porch, the one my mother planted. We use silver sippers, thin silver straws with leaf-shaped spoon bowls at one end, to sip and to swirl the honey idly around the glass.

My father reads the paper; I read a book. Inside, my stepmother is fixing dinner.

When she calls us to the table, I sit down at my father's right hand, my place before the suicide. My stepmother sits at his left hand, in my mother's place. He says grace, insists on holding both my stepmother's hand and my own. He is full of pieties. During dinner he makes pronouncements: "For my money, there's no place like home," or, "You'll never get a meal as good as this in a restaurant." He wants us to know that this time he means it; no one is moving out of this house.

He takes color photographs of the family around the dinner table: my stepmother glaring into the middle distance, my brothers, home on vacation, standing by their chairs, drinks in hand. When I look at these pictures, I see flesh-colored ghosts floating in my mother's dining room. Her pictures on the walls, her china, her furniture, the room itself are more real than we are. But to my father, the photos are evidence for the defense: nothing has ever happened in this house. No one has gotten up and walked into the kitchen to turn on the gas.

I feel a strong sense of empathy with him; I believe I'm the only one in the family who really understands him, who recognizes that it has all been a mistake, that something has gone grievously wrong and he has been unfairly treated. I believe he feels the same thing for me, that he wants to comfort me and that our complicity is his way of doing so.

In fact, though, I'm nothing more than his alibi—the living proof, the spitting image of my mother.

ALL AROUND me, people act as though nothing is going on. Hal has started college, so he's only around during holidays, but his room is full of his books, his records, and his guns; it feels like him. I spend a lot of time up there, listening to jazz and show albums and reading everything from Mickey Spillane to Thomas Mann. Hal seems to feel something, to have some juice. We never talk about our mother, but I believe that because he listens to jazz and collects novels, he is sympathetic. Just reading his books is comforting; I feel safe in his room.

When I'm thirteen I line his gun racks with felt for his Christmas present. When I'm fifteen I read his notes from Carlos Baker's class on Hemingway, read the novels and fall in love with Robert Jordan in *For Whom the Bell Tolls*. When I see the movie, I fall in love all over again with Gary Cooper and Ingrid Bergman; I envy the pleasure they have before death and deprivation overtake them. I read *Death in the Afternoon* and become obsessed with bullfighting. I'm looking for the key to Hemingway's stoicism, his grace under pressure. It seems to me that my father, who has never read Hemingway, who despises novels, would understand and respect his code. My father keeps telling me I have to learn to be tough-minded. He likes to quote Kipling: "If all men count with you, but none too much."

I translate Hemingway and my father into a command not to care about anything. I become a teenage cynic, and write "LIAB," standing for "Life is a Bitch" on my notebooks. But of course I am full of all the normal bruised teenage feelings. Is my conviction of doom, my awareness of a monumental injustice, really any different from the usual adolescent angst? My family doesn't think so; I am easy to tease.

Erik is a high-school junior, the last brother to live full time in the boys' dormitory. He's working hard to keep his rage under control. He busies himself with football and the student council, where he finds a mentor in the faculty adviser. She teaches him to be politic and to give speeches, and she takes him to student-council conventions around the state and country.

Boys drape themselves around the house. In the summers we all go to Martin's Dam. Hal lifeguards. At night he drives around with his friends and his guns; once, when I'm fifteen or sixteen, he and a friend take me out to a roadhouse with them. I look older than my age, and I sit sipping a gin and ginger and listening to the boys talk, all that seems to be required for the appearance of maturity.

My father and stepmother have a real life together, in which she is a match for him; she will never kill herself. When she gets angry, which is frequently, he spends hours mollifying her. She is angry at him for getting home late from work, for working on weekends, for never wanting company. She is angry at me for not coming home right after school to do chores, although if I do come home she is invariably napping and the dinner is prepared, ready to cook, the kitchen immaculate. The kitchen is her power base; she will not allow me to do anything there or in the house, but this somehow enrages her. She says my father and I are both selfish and never think of her. In that, she is partly right. We also exchange glances of commiseration when, stoked with bourbon, she launches one of her dinner-table tirades. When she really gets wound up, she is fond of grand, melodramatic gestures, like threatening to throw all her furniture out the bedroom window, that get my father's attention. Despite my best efforts, her rages terrify me; I know she's mostly drunk, and bluffing, but I'm still afraid she will repay my general ignoring of her tirades and directives with some terrible punishment, as my mother did.

We don't entertain very often, but when we do, or when one of my brothers invites friends for supper, my father is charming; a host. He likes to tell jokes and little moral parables after dinner, standing up in his place at the head of the table, with a cigar in one hand and his smoky gray crystal glass of liqueur in the other. Now that he's married to a Catholic, his jokes take on an ecumenical flavor. He likes stories that involve a Protestant, a Catholic, and a Jew, or a Scotsman, an Irishman, and a Jew. These stories take passing cuts at Protestants and Catholics, or at Scots and Irish, but the punchlines are generally at the expense of the Jews, who aren't represented at the dinner table.

One of his favorite stories, though, is pure Catholic. He must have gotten it from my stepmother, who might have gotten it from a passing nun or priest: A nun goes out on the town and returns to the convent tipsy. When the mother superior calls her in and asks what she has to say for herself, the nun solemnly cocks her finger at the mother superior and says, "Bang! Bang!" Shocked, the mother superior sends the nun to her cell. The next day, she calls the nun up before the whole convent and says, "Sister, I want you to repeat exactly what you said to me last night." The nun cocks her finger at the mother superior and says, "Click.

Click." "Sister," the mother superior says, "last night you said 'Bang! Bang!'" "I know, mother," says the nun, "but last night I was loaded."

ARNO MARRIES his high-school girlfriend. Erik acquires a steady girlfriend. My father has recognized for some time that his sons are growing up. I first realized that things were changing for Hal and Erik, and that my father approved, when a young woman arrived at our house in Baltimore one summer afternoon with a portable record player and a case of records. My father gallantly set up the record player for her on a card table in the corner of the dining room, from which the dining table had been removed to the front hall. I watched while the young woman danced the fox-trot with each of my brothers in turn, showing them the basic step first and then guiding them around the floor. Then she danced with my father, a graceful dancer who mastered the dancing teacher. I watched her give way to him, relaxing her shoulders and knees that had been poised to lead and teach. At the end of the dance he whirled her around fast and pulled her in close, expertly, to stop dead center with the last note. She threw back her head and laughed. Then she went back to teaching my brothers.

I'm a different story. My father isn't going to let me get away. The deal is that as surrogate goddess I belong in my mother's bed; if I live, if I'm free, I'm taking my mother away from him. But because I remind him and my brothers of her, they can never quite forgive me for being alive. So I am to pay for the destruction of my mother's body with the forfeit of my own. For the guilty knowledge and complicity of my father and brothers with the presumption of my own guilt, and my abject need to atone. For their freedom to live their lives in the world with my own entombment at the center of the family. I will be the rememberer so they can forget. I will sacrifice myself so they can live.

I make it easy for them. As adolescence approaches, my body, which I have loved, have counted on to climb trees, to ride my bicycle faster than anyone on the block, to run, to jump, but above all to escape, begins to fail me. At nine, at ten, it was strong and trustworthy, my brain was rational, my habits established. I was in control, at the peak of my powers as a child. I felt cool, worthy. Now I'm facing betrayal.

Did it happen to my mother in the same way? Certainly she forbade my sexuality from the start. Nothing more than the usual stuff girls were subjected to in those days: When she caught me, aged five or six, rubbing myself, and I told her it felt good, then (quickly, to keep it innocent) that I itched, she told me I might have a disease. When my best friend Barbara told her mother that she and I, aged nine, had been looking for pubic hairs, Barbara's mother became hysterical and called my mother, who also became hysterical. Both mothers impressed upon us the awfulness of what we had done, and we were forbidden to spend the night together for some time.

Thousands, maybe millions of girls have had to struggle through similar strictures to arrive at their adult sexuality. But my mother had destroyed her body.

I remember sitting in the bathtub and watching her walk naked from the basin, her copper-colored bush glowing.

Her breasts hung firm and round, her shoulders were straight, her hips broad and womanly, squared off slightly on each side by the jut of the pelvic bone. Her skin was mottled-brown at the nipples, and light-reddish at the wrists and neck, where it was weathered from gardening.

When she died, my own body was still smooth, hairless, breastless, with no signs yet of a change from a neuter child, a girl who, if my hair were cut short, could, in jeans, easily pass for a boy. But I had taken it for granted that someday my mother's body would be mine, that I would grow up, have a life as a woman. As long as she was alive, I didn't have to fear the promise of that future. Then she destroyed her body. Put it in the oven, practically a self-Auschwitz. One of the first things that occurred to me was that if I were a girl, I was going to die.

When sexuality began its work in my body and mind — when I became, inevitably, self-aware and self-conscious — I was terrified. The psychological changes started when I was eleven, in Cranford, before we moved back to St. Davids. I struggled to hang on to my ability to lose myself in make-believe; I remember standing by the lake in the park in front of our little split-level ranch house, trying to make the tacky development disappear in my mind and a medieval king-dom appear, in which I was a squire on my way to knight-hood. I desperately wanted that to be the rite of passage before me; I dreaded the one I faced.

At the same time, I hung out with some older girls who introduced me to *True Confessions* magazine. At summer camp I wore makeup for the first time and got kissed by an older boy who thought I was older, too (I was big for my age) but was quickly disabused by my insistence on keeping my lips pressed firmly together.

For two years I remained suspended between never-never land and the future. But when, at thirteen, in St. Davids, there came the uncontrollable outpouring, the appalling shame of menstruation, I was exiled from make-believe forever.

Of course I knew that menstruation meant I could have babies, and that that was supposed to be a wonderful thing. But I was too burdened by the past; I had been trained to maintain a cool distance from my body, to control it as completely as possible, to feel disgust with its outpourings and fear of its sexual responses. I looked forward to giving birth with as much pleasure as I'd looked forward to menstruation; the possibilities for dissolution were immense. When I discovered that the sight of my fully clothed body could bring boys and men to attention, my flush of excitement and power was undermined by shame and fear.

One afternoon in the first summer of my menstruation I put on a pair of black-and-white houndstooth-check short shorts with a red belt, my padded bra, and a white cotton halter top I have bought with my allowance. Barefoot, I walk across the street, where Tommy Sergeant is washing his father's car in the driveway. I have known Tommy since I was six; he and I have climbed trees, pelted each other with crab apples, even mock-wrestled. I was a kid in the neighborhood, and he was an older kid. Now he's sixteen.

He's leaning across the hood of the car with a can of Simonize in one hand and a rag in the other. He doesn't look up when I stop by the tail of the car. I say, "Hello, Tommy," and he glances at me. Then he looks. Then he stands up and walks over to me and smiles and says hello, standing close enough to look down my halter top. I have carefully arranged it so that he won't, I hope, be able to see the padded bra.

I can feel that his interest in me has nothing to do with what we're saying. I myself am barely aware of the conversation; I'm focusing on my own growing warmth and excitement, the scary pleasure of Tommy Sergeant standing close to me, almost touching my padded bra. I thrust it toward his chest; I feel a challenge is being made, a dare being dared; I feel alive.

And then I walk back across the street to our porch and sit down. It's cooler here in the shade; I'm hidden from the road by bushes but I can see out. Tommy Sergeant's driveway looks a million miles away, a mirage shimmering in the August heat. All my mother's taboos are working inside me; the grim stone house wall behind me belongs to a prison or a tomb. When my father comes home from work, I will have to sit with him on this porch in the twilight. I have seen him with his hands seemingly at my mother's throat, leaning over her, his face red, engorged, his body heaving, her face hanging upside down over the side of the bed, mouth open as if to scream.

It was during the war. He was home from Persia, a complete stranger, a huge dark bulk of a man standing next to my mother on the Nickle Plate platform. She had been excited for weeks, had even repainted their bedroom—which I, in my crib, had been sharing with her in his absence. He kicked me out in stages; first I was moved to a little bed in their room, with the backs of chairs lined up to prevent me from falling out. I don't think he waited to make love to my mother, but all I saw that night was his erection, huge, astonishing, threatening. The next night my bed and I were moved to the room my brother Erik had had to himself. I waited until Erik was asleep, then climbed out of bed and stumped back to my mother's room to reclaim my turf.

The next day, I couldn't take my eyes off my mother; I was amazed that she was walking around, briskly changing sheets, wearing a summer dress, not a mark on her.

It wasn't just Tommy Sergeant and I getting excited in his driveway that summer afternoon when I was thirteen; it was the explosion roaring inside the house, and my mother's body on the ironing board, her face hanging upside down off the end.

As my body matures my family watches me carefully, always ready with prohibitions: *Don't sit with your legs crossed*— my stepmother. *Don't chew gum on the street. Don't push your sleeves up*—Erik, whenever he has to walk anywhere with me. He is extremely conscious of my femininity and extremely critical of my attempts to assert it. The first time I experiment with eye liner, he looks closely at me and announces, "You didn't do it right. No wonder it looks terrible."

My father paraphrases Robert Burns: "If you could only see yourself the way others do!" Implying that I would be as horrified as he was. He takes care to tell me what he thinks of sexually active women. His favorite moral parable, one he especially loves to tell after dinner, is about a man who asks a woman if she'll sleep with him for a million dollars. "Of course," she says. Then he asks her if she'll do it for ten dollars. "What do you think I am?" she says, indignantly. "I know what you are," he says, "I'm just trying to establish your price."

But he loves to flirt; likes me to kiss him on the cheek when he comes home from work, press my lips ever so slightly into its soft, yielding curve, smell the lingering aftershave and say, "You smell nice," so he can flash back, "I am nice." Sometimes, on a summer afternoon, if he catches me on the upstairs landing, on my way out of the house in shorts, he pats me on the bottom and calls me his 'dizzy blonde.' (I have been learning from Hal that the worst thing a woman can be is a cock-teaser, a flirt, but it never occurs to me to accuse my father of sexual teasing; I bask in these little scraps of approval.)

We never buy a television set because my father says he believes in conversation. I go over to a friend's house after school to watch *American Bandstand*. We talk about going into Philadelphia to get on the show, but we never dare. The kids on the screen are South Philly types, the girls chewing gum, wearing tight skirts and tighter angora sweaters, their permed hair swept up in barettes and then falling loose in ringlets. The boys wear their collar-length hair combed into extravagant pompadours in the front and DAs in the back. Their pants are pegged and their shirt collars turned up.

We're Main Line kids in white blouses with Peter Pan collars, circle skirts and loafers. My father calls jitterbugging "sex standing up."

When I'm sixteen or seventeen I bring home a Polaroid snapshot someone has taken at a dance, in which my boyfriend and I are slow-dancing, close, our eyes closed. I tuck the photo in a book on the table next to my bed. One day when I come home from school my stepmother is waiting in the front hall in a rage, holding the photograph: "What do you mean, bringing home a picture like this? Your father will be furious."

Stunned silence. She holds out the photograph. I take it.

"Tear it up," she says.

"No!" I scream, feeling craziness open up around me. My ears are ringing. I try reason: "You had no right to go through my things. This is mine. It's private." I know it's no use; I know she regularly rummages through my room — that even Erik isn't immune from search-and-seizure. I also know that her Irish Catholic soul, while tolerant of drinking, draws the line altogether at sex.

I think, *We weren't doing anything wrong. We were only holding each other close.*

"If you don't tear it up, I'll show it to your father," she says.

Reason crumbles. I tear the picture up.

"Signe, you'll never regret this," she says. I already do.

This is a couple of years after my father drove my stepmother and me to Buzzard's Bay, Cape Cod, for a holiday weekend, all three of us in the same motel room. Early in the morning he woke me up and told me to put on my bathing suit. We reached the dock before I remembered that he and my mother sometimes used to drive out to Martin's Dam for early-morning swims.

I resented the hour and the chill fog; I didn't want to stand beside my father in my bathing suit. He was boyish and flirtatious; he insisted that I dive in first. I was afraid he would land on top of me in the water; as soon as my head came up I started swimming back to the dock. I stood, shivering, wrapped in the skimpy motel towel, while he swam out and back. When he stepped up onto the dock the cloth of his pale yellow bathing suit was pulled tight against the bulge in his crotch. We walked in silence back to the room, where my stepmother sat on the side of the bed smoking a cigarette.

THINGS BEGIN to get very tricky for me. The house is steaming with sexuality: near-naked encounters at the bathroom door and in the hall, bulges of cocks and balls in jockey shorts and jeans; jockstraps, underpants, T-shirts, wet-dream stains on sheets, intimate impedimenta of the laundry basket. My father's morning shave in boxer shorts, the bathroom door half open. Myself, the teenage girl full of juice, of incipient lust, threatening to break out.

My mother's ashes lie buried in her family's plot in a churchyard in Douglaston, Long Island. They're clean, holy, pure, and dead. But I'm heir to her and to her act; in me they might bloom again. The men have made me the arsenal of all that was messy and destructive in her suicide, the repository of all they despise about women. I'm drugged with knowledge, steeped in forbidden sexuality, a prisoner in the wet dreams and nightmares of my father and his sons.

I try never to open my closet door unless I have on a robe or am fully clothed. But sometimes I forget; I open the door wearing only underpants, or a slip, and my father is standing on his side, a dark shadow behind the rows of my clothes and his. He never says anything, but I have the feeling he's been waiting for me.

I ask for a partition between his side of the double closet and mine, but I am ignored; privacy is not supposed to matter to me. At night, if I'm in bed, reading, I never know when anyone will open the door from the hall and walk in. They never knock. So I write savagely satirical pieces about the family and leave them on the desk in my room; I know my stepmother will read them when she goes through my room, looking for evidence.

Years later I read about Lizzie Borden, whose bedroom had four doors, one more than mine; in fact, it seems to have been more a hall landing than a room. It opened directly into both her sister's room and the room where her father slept with her stepmother. Like mine, the doors to her room had no locks; anyone in the family could walk in at any moment of the day or night. I understand the murderous rage with which she used her ax; she was thirty-four years old, and she had never had a moment of privacy.

On Sunday mornings, while my stepmother is downstairs in the kitchen fixing an exact duplicate of the hearty brunches my mother used to serve—waffles and kidney stew, Julekake, the sweet citroned bread we loved hot from the oven all year around, slathered with butter and layered with thin slices of gjetost, the sweet brown goat's milk cheese that was another Norwegian legacy—my father steals upstairs. Hearing his heavy step in the hall, I curl up in fetal position on the far side of the bed, my back to the door. He comes in, sits on the edge of the bed, and leans over me, bracing himself with a stiff-arm to the mattress, his large forearm tight against my smaller ones folded protectively across my breasts. His left hand is heavy on my shoulder. He speaks caressingly: "Won't you get up now, Signe? Nona's fixing a wonderful breakfast, just for us." As he speaks, he leans over until I can feel his breath on my cheek, his arm pressing against me.

I barely breathe; I pretend to be deeply asleep and lie there in silence until he gives up and goes downstairs. Or I produce a noncommittal grunt that he takes for assent. Then he gives me a squeeze before leaving. Either way, after he leaves shame overcomes me. I can't bear the knowledge, my sense of complicity. Isn't lying there asking for it? Shouldn't I get up early and be ready for him, dressed? Isn't there a secret excitement in the knowledge of what's between us?

The truth is, he has me. He's an artist, careful to keep my stepmother the public body in his bed. Only he and I know about Sunday mornings, when he's alone with me on the bed he shared with my mother, trying to seduce me awake.

I BECOME hopelessly embroiled in the family version; I wonder whether I have been born a bad seed, germinating and growing in the heart of this happy family. The faces of my father and brothers, even of my stepmother, become a set of mirrors that show me countless magnified images of my worst fears about myself: Troublemaker. Murderer. A monstrous failure and narcissist whose incapacities and countless thoughtless, unearned, willful, self-centered acts have fatally disappointed, wounded the saint.

The mirrors reveal me as a warped and tainted image of my dead mother — a constant, painful reminder to everyone, including myself, of the more perfect person whose death I have caused. I come to realize that I have no right to take up any space of my own within the family. In fact, I'm a nonperson; by rights I should not be alive at all.

How can I occupy her bed, use her closet, keep my things in her drawers? If I have dared hope I might in some way replace her in the house, the truth is that I never can. She has passed into myth, become a fiction. I am no longer the heroine of my own play; I have become a character in hers.

FOURTEEN

Final Analysis

A FTER THAT, it was impossible for me to escape just by leaving home. I was in too deep.

At college, as I've said, the suicide kept working inside me. So did my self hatred. I reacted to ordinary events in ways that made no sense to me at all: I met a boy in Harvard Yard and agreed to go out with him, but when he called the dorm I panicked and tried desperately to find someone else to take my place. Responses that someone with insight or merely forbearance might have forgiven herself for drove me crazy until I had somehow corrected or at least compensated for them. The spring of my freshman year I fell in love with a boy some friends introduced me to, but when he wanted sex a few weeks after we met I was afraid. I lost him, of course. So that summer at the shore I went out and lost my virginity to a stranger I picked up in a bar. There are ways to write about this that would make it sound amusing, but in fact I was drunk beforehand and depressed for days afterward.

School provided moments of great pleasure, reading Milton and Chaucer and Shakespeare or conquering some difficult course. But I couldn't see myself as a scholar. I believed I was a writer—although I knew absolutely that I had no right to be one.

My father never forgave me for choosing to go to college in another state. He wanted me to go to the local Seven Sisters school and live with him and my stepmother. When I left college at the end of the first semester of my sophomore year, sunk in depression, he was triumphant; he thought he had won me back, that I had come home to stay for good in the apartment on Rittenhouse Square in Philadelphia into which he and my stepmother had moved.

It was my stepmother who kept me going to a psychiatrist until I could focus myself enough to leave again. This second defection made my father so angry that he threw me out of the family so I would have to use up a small inheritance from my great-aunt to return to school. I suppose he was hoping I would give up and stay home, but I didn't. I set myself grimly to finish school. Once I had graduated, an occasion he never acknowledged, I stopped going home even to visit.

That didn't help. If I wouldn't go back, I couldn't move on, either. I was stuck. My emotions weren't giving me any useful information; I was full of pity and benevolence for my family, and I was still incredibly depressed.

Eventually, after my father's death, I found an analyst I

trusted. She was sympathetic, but it took a long time for things to come out. My family was more extreme than she was at first able to recognize, and for quite a while I could only tell her as much as I consciously knew, or thought. My ideas had been shaped by the nicely dovetailing imperatives of my family, which had taught me that complaints are unacceptable because they mean I'm thinking about myself, and of the culture, which decrees that growing up means coming to terms with your parents. So I tried to keep a stiff upper lip about my family; I had developed a plausible, Potemkin-Village version of maturity.

Nevertheless, by a combination of my resistance and the analyst's trying out her hunches, we progressed. From the start I was sure of some things. For instance, the analyst once suggested that I might have been able to get more attention from my mother if I had worked a little harder at it. This caused me much distress; finally I said that my mother didn't have any more attention to give than she had given, and that I had known this very early on. What would have been the point of trying for what wasn't there?

About many other things, I was full of confusion; although my father was dead, I was still desperately making excuses for him. I believed I had certainly loved him, as I had loved my mother, and they had both loved me. I loved my brothers, too, and I was still looking for their approval. I thought I understood them all so well that the question of forgiveness didn't even arise. I thought that at some level we must all be in sympathy, because we had been through the same thing.

Eventually I learned, painfully, that I had piled all this

love and understanding and need and fear into a kind of large watertight compartment I occupied in my mind, shored up against the memories and the emotions I kept hidden in a whole series of equally watertight compartments underneath. Of course you can never really keep feelings hidden, except from yourself. Anger came out all the time, as the generalized hostility that was characteristic of my family, and as bouts of pure rage when I was alone in my apartment. In those bouts, objects usually took the brunt of my feelings—the telephone suffered fractures, and my tin pan lids still bear the scars of hammer blows. For a while, when I lived in a railroad flat, with rooms laid out end-to-end like a railroad train, I would stand in my bedroom doorway and hurl eggs and the occasional plate through the kitchen to smash against the bathroom wall above the tub. But when things got particularly frustrating I would skip the constructive substitutes and go directly to my head, hitting it with the flat of my hand or my fists or banging it against the wall.

Luckily I broke out of my watertight compartment before I broke my head. Underneath it the other compartments were waiting; when I fell into the first one, I discovered my life with my mother before she killed herself. That was when I began to think about this book. It took twelve more years to recover enough of my memories, and of myself, to finish writing it.

I'm older now than my mother was when she killed herself; perhaps that means I've escaped her fate. My analyst has succeeded in keeping me alive, always her first aim even when I didn't see the point of it. Suicide is seductive;

when it becomes an option, you toy with the idea of it. It's always there, the ultimate self-hurting, the ultimate revenge. For years, whenever I believed I had screwed everything up I would think I had to commit suicide; there didn't seem to be anything else to do with myself. This mood can still come on me, but it's rarer now.

The "I" who would kill myself clearly isn't quite the same "I" who is writing this book. I think of my killer self as some kind of fascist, descendant of an Inquisitor, an absolutist who judges by rigid standards of unattainable perfection. He (somehow I always think of this self as a he, perhaps because, in my experience, a woman may judge a child but a man is always the ultimate judge of that woman) is detached, a critical observer who misses nothing. He may look harmless, leaning up against a wall, arms folded, smiling skeptically, one eyebrow raised, ready with some cutting remark about my performance. But when the time comes to denounce me, he is cold, clinical, merciless. He may be a *kapo,* a fellow inmate turned straw boss, who does the dirty work for the Nazis who run the camp. Like any servant, he is more rigid than his masters; his narcissistic rage is aroused by the slightest defection from the rules.

I also see this killer self as an abused infant grown to adult tyrant, a monster who demands instant, perfect harmony with its own fantasies and desires. It is descended from a long line of emotionally starved infants, each one in turn encouraged, by way of compensation, to become one of the tyrants who abused it in the first place. In every generation the abuse was nothing more than what passed for ordinary childrearing, just as it was in my life and in my mother's.

The self I would kill is, of course, the scapegoat, the victim, the irredeemable fuck-up everyone, including me, has given up for lost. The abused infant herself, the one who hasn't yet become a fascist. She feels a lot more like me than the killer, but, like any good German, when she's committed some offense I have to dissociate myself from her. So purity, offended, can burn away dross, the Calvinist soul refine itself. We had to torch this village to save it.

In short, I embraced both possibilities of self offered in my family. All my life these two selves have existed in a terrible dialectic; the fascist defining the scapegoat, the scapegoat justifying, indeed necessitating, the fascist. Barring a miracle, the fascist would long ago have done in the scapegoat.

I've been extraordinarily lucky; I've had that miracle. My analyst has had the patience to listen to me for more years than most people would believe could possibly be necessary, the wisdom to help me discover my reality in ways that haven't totally overwhelmed me, and the love to support me rather than tear me down. She has not only kept me from killing myself, she has suggested the possibility of living, as opposed to merely not dying. In the process she's become something very like the mother I never had. It's been a long time since I've beaten myself over the head.

My dead mother still frightens me, though. I think she was irrevocably split between killer and victim, and so was only occasionally and tenuously in possession of something, or someone, that could be called her own self. That's why she's so hard to describe, so elusive; most of the time she was simply not there. I don't even know who she might have been, except that she almost certainly would have taken pleasure in her crafts, in potting and printmaking as well as in breadmaking and gardening. Being able to take pleasure, she would not have been so frightening. She would have been able to live with herself, so she might have liked me. And she might very well still be alive—her own mother lived to be ninety-three.

Instead she was incarcerated in the concentration camp of the soul. Where, as *kapo,* she had to kill her fellow inmate, herself.

I THINK that what was going on in my mother's head just before she killed herself was a continuation of the drama she had played out with me in Fort Wayne, when I was very small and she was driven to fury by my impulses and desires. Her rage then had been as much at herself as at me, because she saw me as part of herself. It was as if, in the face of my two-year-old needs, her fragile, hard-won sense of selfhood, of body-and-mind integrity, broke down, and she was overwhelmed by an avatar of her helpless infant self. In an act beyond empathy, denying all boundaries of age, of body, of size, of self, she *became* me, and I became her. She would make me perfect, because she couldn't endure imperfection in a piece of herself.

I was split by her madness. To survive, I took her path, on which, in conscious life, the good and the bad selves never meet. When she started out on that path, who had broken her? Was it her mother, that tiny, gentle survivor I knew? Someone must have set her on it. Yet she grew up, and married, and was thought to be an ordinary human being, a woman who had chosen her life, much like any other woman.

How can we know, in the wheel of the self, what we have chosen and what is forced upon us? And why, when so much else is possible, are we doomed to live with choices made in terror and desperation, at an age so young the selves we make can never fit the fabric of a later, larger life?

WHEN I think of my mother in relation to my father, he is always the killer and she is always the victim. This is perhaps unfair to him, but I can't get away from the fact that as a man he had a sense of entitlement that my mother could never have; although he certainly learned as a child to suppress himself in many ways, his world gave him ample compensation. His indirect expressions of himself were rich and varied, and always at someone else's expense. His grievances against his mother—who, in the tradition of macho societies everywhere, was powerful and demanding and saw her eldest boy as a prince—could be played out in his relationship with other women his whole life long. He was offered ambition and given the services of a woman to help him achieve his goals. He was expected to make outrageous demands on this woman, and he did. He was free to indulge in the tyranny of a monstrous baby determined to be coddled at all cost. He was not expected to inquire as to his wife's needs or desires; she was his moveable feast, his permanent floating Rest & Rehabilitation resort.

Which brings me to the element of revenge. On one level,

it was straightforward: My mother brought my father down with her. If she felt he was demanding that she sacrifice her lifelong goal just as she had finally achieved it—or, worse, that he was completely unaware of what the house in St. Davids meant to her—she was certainly astute enough about social and workplace politics to realize that her suicide would be a blot on his record. If he had rendered all her years of sacrifice futile, she made all his years of striving a waste.

I think she had a more primitive revenge motive as well, one I'm familiar with, that used to inspire my own suicide mood when I was out of sorts with the universe—when I wanted to say, "There! *Now* you'll believe I was serious!" When I wanted to prove to people that I mattered to them, that they would care when I'm gone.

This is the cry of the unnurtured self. It's considered childish, and I suppose it is; it's the scapegoat's fantasy, just as suicide is the scapegoat's mode. Killing oneself is never a solo act; it's always a collaboration between scapegoat and fascist, the end result of an unconscious dialogue between victim and killer.

I also think my mother was killing my father when she killed herself, so closely did she identify him with her own killer self, so totally did he play into that identification with his own manipulative and implacable being. She couldn't have bargained on his remarrying so soon, and spending the rest of his life pretending, at my expense, that nothing had ever happened. I don't really think she meant her vengeance to extend to me.

But it did, precisely because she did stop my father in his

tracks. Behind his life with his second wife, behind the
ruins of his career, he loitered in his secret kingdom, his
shrine, his second temple, with me, his surrogate goddess,
as its altarpiece. After I got away, he lived out his last few
years in the apartment with my stepmother. He died of a
coronary aneurysm in 1966, soon after his sixty-third birthday. Even my brothers and sisters-in-law, I've been told,
were relieved.

SINCE COLLEGE my life, too, has both gone on and not
gone on. There have been lovers, and jobs, and books and
articles written, and causes fought for. There's been a life, of
sorts, in the arts: performing in avant-garde dance-theater
in the halcyon sixties, when we believed we were going to
remake the world; writing poetry and reading it in the bars
when there was still a lively poetry scene in the city. I've
published four books, many articles, some poetry, and a few
stories. I've been an editor in book publishing and on a
national magazine.

The whole time I've thrown myself into causes, partly
because I've believed in them and partly because they're
useful for someone who can't live with herself but has a lot
of energy and a strong need for commitment. I marched in
Boston against the segregationist School Committee and on
Washington to hear Martin Luther King say he had a dream.
During the Vietnam War I made antiwar street theater and
helped produce antiwar theatrical events for Angry Arts
and marched on Washington several more times.

In the heady days of feminism I helped organize the sit-in

at the *Ladies' Home Journal* that won us a special supplement
in which to spread the word to the heartland. I wrote a piece
for that supplement and helped run the tumultuous meeting
that decided which feminist interest groups were going to
get the money we earned for it. I met with my New York
Radical Feminists consciousness-raising group and helped
start new ones, marched down Fifth Avenue in the euphoric
feminist parade, picketed here and there and liberated a bar
or two.

As a junior trade book editor, bored because young
women were still supposed to be seen and not heard from, I
ran the house union until I was fired for organizing the
publisher's textbook division. Years later I helped start a
national writers' union and develop it for a year and a half
until the opposition staged a coup so it could demolish
everything we had built and start all over again on its own
terms.

All these experiences greatly enlarged my political education. But I didn't practice the politics of pushing poetry,
or any kind of writing that felt like it belonged to me rather
than to the market for which I had written it, into a career
that would also feel like an identity. At the crucial moments
I always retreated, into a limbo where my secret seemed
safe. I did the same thing in relationships; I neither married
nor had children.

Where did I disappear to? Nowhere, like my mother.
Overwhelmed by fear, I sought its antidote, perfection:
perfect beauty or perfect contemplation or perfect distance
or perfect behavior. Maybe I thought my mother would be
there, too. Like her, I could not face the consequences of

failure or imperfection. Equally, I feared the damage I believed I would do if I were successful, the reprisals I believed would inevitably follow. My retreat was a kind of demi or symbolic suicide, an abdication from myself and from the limitations and possibilities of reality.

My shrink keeps telling me I'm entitled, but I still more than half-believe that every act of self-assertion is one of murderous rage, because if I exist someone else—my mother—can't. Anger is certainly murderous; to say I was angry at my mother is as good as saying I wanted her dead. I did, many times, but I never expected my wish to be granted.

Rage is pure reaction; understanding takes distance and hard-won knowledge. It doesn't cancel anger out, although we would like it to. It tempers the expression of the raw emotion, but the infant has still got to be fed somehow. Our family has never been any good at that. I've noticed, for instance, that my uncle could never say directly that he wanted to do something. He always had to persuade my aunt, or a relative or visitor such as myself, to say *she* wanted to do it, so he could accommodate her. He believed he must always defer to a woman, had no right to a simple desire of his own, while the women in the family have always felt they must defer to the men. That causes resentment all around, and no end of manipulation.

If you could ask any of the men in the family why he can't be direct, and he could tell you the truth, he would say that he's afraid he will be turned down. Worse; that he will be teased, ridiculed, belittled. So he learned to despise needs as a sign of weakness, never acknowledging the anger boiling underneath. Since I was raised in the same tradition—teased, ridiculed, and belittled in my turn—I have the same fear of rejection, learned the same rejection of anger. But my mother's suicide forcefully underlined for me the existence and the power of that unacknowledged fury. My rage and my needs are so linked in my mind that my fear of one is the same as my fear of the other.

Still, although I'm cursed with both my mother's anxiety and its drug, perfectionism, the fascist in my head is shrinking. Sometimes I feel he has been reduced to a tiny figure—still screaming, not yet comic, not yet quite a *Hogan's Heroes* Nazi, but futile at last.

And if I have always retreated, given way to my fears, I have always emerged to try again, right up to that moment of commitment, the declaration of *I am*.

Which I have now made. It's time to forgive myself.

MY BROTHERS and I all keep cats, because our mother was fond of cats and we grew up with them, as she did. Petting our cats gives us the feeling that physical affection is still a possibility. Those of us who have children didn't pet those children when they were small, any more than our mother petted us. The cats give it to us vicariously, as they did when she was alive.

As a child, I was consumed with the idea that there should be equal time for everybody. At night I would line up my dolls and stuffed animals so each one would get time next to my body. There was room for one on each side of me in bed; the rest lay on the floor in a row that extended, perpendicular to the plane of my body, from the bed out across the room.

Each night I would put the one that had been farthest out on the floor the night before onto the bed. For that night and the one following it would enjoy the bliss of sleeping next to my body, first on the wall side, then on the outer side. Then it would begin again its slow journey to the limbo of distance, staring straight up from the floor, unable even to see me. I, if I chose, might lean to see it, but sometimes I did not choose to. It pleased me to be remote.

When I think of my mother, she is always alone, too, even when I am with her. Her back is turned, or her head averted. Sometimes I still wish I could muscle in on her scene and force her to acknowledge me, because maybe then she would change her mind.